Low Allergy Food, the Tasty Way

Anita Kennedy

Low Allergy Food, the Tasty Way

iUniverse®

LOW ALLERGY FOOD, THE TASTY WAY

iUniverse books may be ordered through booksellers or by contacting:

iUniverse
1663 Liberty Drive
Bloomington, IN 47403
www.iuniverse.com
1-800-Authors (1-800-288-4677)

ISBN: 978-1-5320-4281-2 (sc)
ISBN: 978-1-5320-4283-6 (hc)
ISBN: 978-1-5320-4282-9 (e)

Library of Congress Control Number: 2018902373

Print information available on the last page.

iUniverse rev. date: 03/16/2018

Contents

Recipes are low in salicylate and exclude:

egg

tomato

onion

beef

gelatin

potato

yeast

Introduction

I know what it is like to suffer from both food intolerances and life-threatening allergies (in this case, to egg, tomato, onion, beef, gelatin, potato and yeast). And yet I also know what it is like to make a wide range of delicious meals without these products.

I suffered from salicylate intolerance for more than 30 years, and was frequently plagued with the chore of altering my diet. I managed to cope quite well, cheating every now and then with high-salicylate food, and managing to avoid severe reactions.

As an adult, I suffered from Fibromyalgia Syndrome (from which I was later miraculously healed – *see below*), and took anti-inflammatory medication for nearly four years. This medication appears to have altered my body's response to certain foods.

The first indication of severe food allergies was an anaphylactic reaction to an aspirin product, requiring an intensive care ambulance and a trip to hospital. Through various tests over many months, I was found to be allergic to all the ingredients noted above. In the following years, I became so acutely allergic to onion and tomato that the faintest odor of these foods caused anaphylaxis, and was usually followed by a trip to hospital.

When you suffer from either food allergies or intolerances, you can usually find some substitutes, even though it can be troublesome. When suffering from both, it is even more difficult, but let me assure you that it is not impossible. To my astonishment, there was a genuine lack of reliable material available for food allergy sufferers to use to alter their diets; except, of course, the obvious advice of simply avoiding the trigger. Some resources were catering for only one or two triggers, and others were produced by people who actually knew little about food allergies.

While having firm data on the seven triggers for my allergic reactions was crucial, the fact they were such commonly-used ingredients caused no end of difficulty trying to rid them completely from my pantry. A time of melancholy was followed by the practical reality of getting on with life – "adapt and overcome", as my husband advised me. There were several requirements for the recipes that I developed over the next year, and which I am sure are relevant to the majority of readers:

- Obviously, each recipe must be totally devoid of allergy-producing foods;
- Where possible, safe substitutes are used;
- The result must be nutritious and suited to everyone in the household – cooking separate meals for me alone was not an option; and
- The recipe must be simple enough that anyone in my family – children included – can follow it.

The result was a triumph for me and proved that no matter what life throws at us, we can adapt and overcome. As they say, the proof was not only 'in the pudding', but also in the soups, the salads, the meat dishes, the pastas, and so on. None of the meals that I prepared from this collection led to an allergic reaction.

Fellow sufferers of food allergies, I want you to know that delicious meals and foods are available. In the modern era of fast food and pre-prepared frozen meals and so on, almost all of which carry one of the seven food allergy triggers, you will probably soon discover that your own kitchen is the safest place for meals. Given the growing health issues brought on by poor food choices, being drawn back to your own kitchen is probably a 'silver lining' in our situation.

This collection of recipes covers practically every category of food that you could require – everything from breakfast meals, entrees and main meals to desserts and baking. I hope they give you inspiration to create your own recipes or simply to adapt existing recipes to suit your own needs.

I wish you all the best on your journey and hope you find this collection of recipes helpful.

Miraculous healing in 2016

On 7 February 2016, at our regular church service at Gateway Baptist Church, Mackenzie in Brisbane, one of our pastors offered to pray for healing for anyone in the congregation. Given I had experienced healing before, I believed it was possible. As Pastor Derek prayed for me, I felt covered in God's love and power, and tears began streaming from my eyes. I knew in my heart that I was healed then and there, but Derek advised to proceed cautiously and test trigger foods.

I first tested with tomato sauce, gradually bringing a bottle closer and closer to me until I both smelled and touched, and then tasted it successfully. I am sure you can imagine my elation when I discovered that I was truly healed. I was still cautious about testing onion, and it happened by accident after some was added to a Subway roll I was eating. My excitement was uncontainable. I made a commitment to still publish this book for all those of you who haven't been blessed by healing yet.

Another health hurdle

Unfortunately, I was diagnosed in 2017 with lipoedema and must now work towards an alternative dietary plan to manage the condition. I will attack this problem with the same zest as I did with food allergies.

Anita Kennedy

Measuring conventions
and abbreviations

All measuring conventions used in this book are standard, catering for both metric and imperial systems. They are limited in order to simplify the process and reduce the need for a drawer full of measuring devices:

- *Cup* is generally consistent (usually 240-250 millilitres or 8.75 fluid ounces) for liquid and dry measures in most countries. As it is so useful for the volumes of ingredients in this book, I have decided to use it in spite of the minor variation across countries, and it is unlikely this small difference will cause any real issues.
- *Millilitres* (ml) and *litres* (L) are used for metric volume measures, while *fluid ounces* (fl oz) and *quarts* are used for Imperial volume measures.
- *Teaspoon* (tsp) is consistent across most countries for liquid and dry measures.
- *Grams* (g) and *ounces* (oz) cater for weight measures in every country.

The tablespoon measure is not used in this book because it varies too greatly, and will affect the outcome of the recipes. In Australia, one tablespoon is equal to four teaspoons (20ml / 0.7 fl oz); whereas in other countries, it is equal to three teaspoons (15ml / 0.5 fl oz).

As a quick reference for volume measures, use the following conversions which are approximate only. The small differences are insignificant for these recipes.

Imperial (approximate)	Metric (approximate)	
0.15 fl oz	1 teaspoon	5 ml
0.3 fl oz	2 teaspoons	10 ml
0.5 fl oz	3 teaspoons (1 non-Australian tablespoon)	15 ml
0.7 fl oz	4 teaspoons (1 Australian tablespoon)	20 ml
1 fl oz	8 teaspoons	30 ml
2 fl oz	12 teaspoons = ¼ cup	60 ml
2.7 fl oz	16 teaspoons = ⅓ cup	80 ml
4 fl oz	24 teaspoons = ½ cup	120 ml
8 fl oz	1 cup	250 ml
1 quart	4 cups	1 L

The following tables are ready references for weight measures showing approximate conversions, but which are close enough for these recipes:

Imperial	Metric	Metric	Imperial
0.5 oz	15 g	10 g	0.3 oz
1 oz	30 g	25 g	0.8 oz
2 oz	60 g	50 g	1.75 oz
4 oz	115 g	100 g	3.5 oz
8 oz	225 g	250 g	8.75 oz
16 oz / 1 pound	450 g	500 g	17.6 oz

For more precise conversions, there are some excellent websites to use. For example:

www.exploratorium.edu/cooking/convert/

Cooking temperatures and power settings

Microwave power used for these recipes is 1100 watts (W). The ratings used in these recipes are:

High	1100W or 100%
Medium-high	825W or 75%
Medium	550W or 50%
Low	330W or 30%

Heat temperatures are converted between metric and Imperial measures as follows:

Imperial	Metric
250° Fahrenheit (F)	130° Celsius (C)
300° F	150° C
350° F	180° C
400° F	200° C
450° F	230° C

Packaging sizes may differ

I have created these recipes using locally-available ingredients. Some of these are available in tins and sizes in Australia, but perhaps not in the same quantities elsewhere. Rarely is an ingredient's precise quantity so critical to a recipe, so feel free to find the closest quantity in your local area. You might have to experiment with the amounts, but experimentation is half the fun of cooking.

Vanilla

Some confusion exists for the terms "extract", "essence" and "flavouring" when referring to vanilla. The variability actually relates to the amount of alcohol mixed with the vanillin. The alcohol is used to extract the vanillin from the vanilla bean, and some of this alcohol may be left in final product. To spare readers any confusion, recipes in this book use only "pure vanilla", which typically has only 2-3% alcohol content.

Readers who want to use a formula diluted with alcohol will need to increase the amount of liquid used in the recipe. For example, a 50/50 dilution will require double the amount of liquid used for the recipe so that the required amount of actual vanillin is maintained. On the other hand, readers who use a concentrated solution of vanillin will need to reduce the amount used in the recipes.

Foods of many names

The problem with names of foods is that they are neither used nor available universally, and so some clarification or substitution may be necessary. Several vegetables in recipes in this book need a mention here. In every case, you must ensure that the vegetable you use is appropriate to your allergies or intolerances.

The word "**shallot**" in Australia refers to the plant known scientifically as *Allium fistulosum*, which is from the group of plants which gives us the onion and similar plants used in cooking around the world. Most noticeably, the shallot does not develop an obvious bulb and its leaves are hollow. (The leaves are not often used in this book.)

There seems to be several plants similar to shallots used for cooking, as well as a variety of names for *Allium fistulosum*, and the following should be a comprehensive list of alternative names and suggested alternative plants:

> Baby onion, Bunching onion, Chinese onion, Chinese scallion, Cibol, Egyptian onion, Escallion, Gibbon, Green onion, Green shallot, Japanese bunching onion, Long onion, Onion stick, Oriental onion, Precious

onion, Salad onion, Scallion, Shallot, Spring onion, Stone leek, Syboe, Top onion, Topsetting onion, Tree onion, Walking onion, Welsh onion, Yard onion.

The "shallot (green onion / spring onion / scallion / bunching onion)" (as it is referenced in this book) provided me a suitable alternative to the common onion (*Allium cepa*), and is therefore used frequently in this book. Because we are dealing with potentially life-threatening allergies, it is critical that readers ensure that this is a safe alternative to the common onion. Your local physician or food allergy association should be able to provide a structured method to safely test the suitability of any food substitute. It is possible that other members of the Allium (onion) genus might offer other substitutes for readers, once tested fully.

A wonderful fruit used in recipes in this book is the **choko**. Although available in many countries, many people outside of Australia would not recognise the name, but may be familiar with one of these:

Chayote, Cho-cho, Chouchoute, Christophene / Christophine, Guisquil, Merleton / mirliton, Pear squash, Pipinola, Sayote, Vegetable pear.

In this book, I refer to it as "choko (chayote / mirliton / christophene)".

Spreads, Sauces & Condiments

Cashew Spread
Cheese and Bacon Spread
Chive and Spring Onion Dip
Chocolate Fudge Sauce
Chutney - Pear and Choko/Chayote
Chutney - Mango
Garlic Kebab Sauce and Salad Dressing
Pear Jam/Jelly
Super Salad Dressing
White Sauce

Cashew Spread

1 cup roasted and salted cashews
*¼ tsp butter **or** sunflower oil*

1. Puree cashew nuts in a grinder or food processor until fine and starting to clump.
2. Add oil or butter, and mix through.
3. Use immediately or store in an airtight container in refrigerator.
4. Remove from fridge before use to allow it to soften slightly for easier spreading.

Cheese and Bacon Spread

*¼ cup diced bacon **or** 2 cooked bacon slices/rashers (to be diced after cooking)*
¾ cup grated cheese
1 shallot (green onion / spring onion / scallion / bunching onion) – white part, finely chopped
1 cup thickened gelatin-free cream

1. Fry bacon.
2. If using slices/rashers, cut finely once cooked.
3. Add grated cheese and shallot to pan and melt cheese.
4. Add cream to bind together.
5. Serve in a small bowl.

Serving Suggestion:

As a warm or cooled spread on yeast-free crackers, on soda bread, or as a dip with sticks of celery or blanched fresh green beans.

Chive and Spring Onion Dip

1 shallot (green onion / spring onion / scallion / bunching onion) – white part, diced finely
1 tsp garlic – minced
2-3 stalks of chives – diced finely
1½ cups gelatin-free sour cream
8 tsp egg-free mayonnaise

1. Gently combine all ingredients
2. Chill in the refrigerator until ready to serve.

Chocolate Fudge Sauce

This is truly the best-ever fudge sauce and definitely worth the effort. I cook this in a saucepan rather than the microwave as it is easier and produces a more consistent result. It is delicious over ice-cream, pancakes, and banana, or pretty much whatever takes your fancy. Any leftover sauce can be refrigerated and re-warmed when needed in the microwave.

1 cup gelatin-free cream
½ tsp pure vanilla
60g (2oz) unsalted butter
100g (3.5oz) dark chocolate – chopped or grated
¾ cup brown sugar
8 tsp white sugar
½ cup cocoa powder – sifted

1. In a 2 litre (2 quarts) saucepan, bring the cream, vanilla and butter to the boil.
2. Add the dark chocolate and sugars, stirring until dissolved.
3. Remove saucepan from the heat.

4. Add the cocoa powder, and stir to combine.
5. Return the saucepan to the heat and stir approximately 30 seconds until the mixture comes to the boil.
6. Cool slightly before placing into sterilised jars or a microwavable container.

Chutney - Pear and Choko/Chayote

This chutney is a staple and used in many other recipes to give a wonderful flavour. I often double the recipe because I use it so often.

825g (29oz) chopped canned pears in syrup
½ choko (chayote / mirliton / christophene) – peeled, cored and diced
½ cup brown sugar
4 tsp malt vinegar
½ tsp citric acid
2 stalks of celery – diced
1 leek – diced
3-5 of 500ml (16 fl oz) sterilized preserve jars

1. Bring the pear syrup and choko to boil in a large, heavy-based saucepan.
2. Continue cooking until syrup is reduced by half.
3. Add remaining ingredients to pan and reduce heat to simmer for 10-15 minutes or until thickened.
4. Pour into sterilized jars with lids and refrigerate.

Chutney - Mango

This is not a salicylate-free recipe, but great for days when you want a little treat on the side. Only eat this if it is safe for your salicylate threshold.

2 cups water
½ cup brown sugar
4-6 large ripe mangos – pureed
4 tsp malt vinegar
½ tsp citric acid
2 stalks of celery – diced
1 shallot (green onion / spring onion / scallion / bunching onion) – white part, diced
3-4 of 500ml (16 fl oz) sterilized preserve jars

1. Bring the water and sugar to the boil in a large, heavy-based saucepan.
2. Continue cooking until this syrup is reduced by half.
3. Add remaining ingredients to pan and reduce heat to simmer for 10-15 minutes or until thickened.
4. Pour into sterilized jars with lids and refrigerate.

Garlic Kebab Sauce and Salad Dressing

¼ cup gelatin-free Greek or plain yoghurt
4 tsp gelatin-free sour cream
1 tsp minced garlic

1. Blend all ingredients together.
2. Store in an air-tight container (or sauce bottle) in the refrigerator.

Pear Jam / Jelly

2 cans (825g / 29oz) of pears in syrup – drained and pureed
3 cups white sugar
50g (1.75oz) sachet of pectin for setting jams (for example, Jamsetta® in Australia)
2-3 of 500ml (16 fl oz) sterilized preserve jars

1. Heat the pears on low heat in a heavy-based saucepan.
2. Add sugar and the pectin, and stir until dissolved.
3. Increase heat and bring to the boil for approximately 5 minutes, stirring occasionally.
4. Allow to cool for about 10 minutes and pour into sterilized jars.
5. This is best stored in the refrigerator.

Super Salad Dressing

This delicious dressing will keep refrigerated in an air-tight container for approximately 1 week.

30g (1oz) butter
1 -2 shallots (green onion / spring onion / scallion / bunching onion) – sliced
*1 clove crushed garlic **or** 1-2 tsp minced garlic*
1 tsp malt vinegar
1 cup double gelatin-free cream
2 tsp chopped chives

1. Melt butter in a medium-sized saucepan over medium heat.
2. Add shallots, garlic and malt vinegar and continue to cook.
3. Simmer for 5 minutes.
4. Stir in the cream and chives and simmer uncovered for 10 minutes or until mixture reduces and thickens.
5. Set aside to cool completely.

White Sauce

100g (3.5oz) butter
⅔ cup plain flour
2-2¼ cups milk

1. Place butter into a 1 litre (1 quart) microwave-safe jug or bowl and cook at a MEDIUM-HIGH (75%) setting until the butter is melted – approximately 1 minute, depending on your microwave oven's specifications.
2. Add the flour and stir, until totally combined.
3. Slowly stir in the milk.
4. Cook in the microwave on HIGH (100%) in bursts of 30 seconds, stirring in between, until it reaches a thick saucy texture. (The total time could be around 3 minutes.)

Tip:

Add 1 cup of grated cheese for a cheesy white sauce, add shallots (also known as green onion, spring onion, scallion, bunching onion) and other vegetables or cooked egg-free pasta like macaroni. This sauce is great for lasagne. Also, try a little parsley in the sauce and serve over steamed or poached cod fillets.

Breakfast Dishes

Bacon Wrap
Pancakes
Porridge with Pear for One
Sweetened Porridge for One

Bacon Wrap

Serves 1

2 slices/rashers of rind-less bacon
1 flour tortilla – see recipe in the 'Dough, Pastries and Batters' section
*Margarine **or** Cream cheese **or** Ricotta cheese as a spread*
1 slice of your favourite cheese
Lettuce

1. Gently fry bacon slices/rashers to desired crispness.
2. Warm a tortilla for 10 seconds on HIGH (100%) in the microwave.
3. Cover the tortilla with your chosen spread while warm.
4. Top with cooked bacon and lettuce.
5. Roll up and serve.

Tip:

Before serving, wrap the roll in non-stick baking paper and toast in a sandwich toaster until the cheese is melted.

Pancakes

Serves 4-6

100g (3.5oz) butter - melted
4 tsp baking powder – see recipe in the 'Baking' section
¼ cup sunflower oil
¼ cup water
2 cups milk
3 cups self-raising flour
½ cup white sugar
Optional: ¼ cup choc chips

1. In a large bowl, add the ingredients in the order listed.
2. Beat lightly with a rotary beater until no lumps are visible.
3. Heat a frypan to approximately 180°C/350°F or until a drop of water 'dances' around the pan.
4. Use approximately ¼ of the mixture per pancake.
5. Turn the pancake when bubbles break in the middle of it.
6. Cook the second side until the middle springs back when pressed lightly with a finger.
7. Place onto a plate while the pancake is hot and serve with your favourite toppings.

Tips and suggestions:

Over-beating will result in a tougher pancake. Leftover mixture can be refrigerated for a few days for later use.

Try topping with sifted icing sugar and pure maple syrup and a scoop of ice-cream, or perhaps try lime syrup (see recipe in the 'Icing and Toppings' section).

If you are watching your waistline, try substituting the ½ cup of sugar with 1 tsp of stevia powder mixed with 1 tsp pure vanilla.

Porridge with Pear for One

Serves 1

⅓ cup rolled oats
⅔ cup cold water
1 peeled pear or 2 canned pear halves – chopped or pureed
Milk to taste

1. Place oats and water into a microwave-safe bowl.
2. Cook in the microwave on HIGH (100%) for 1 minute, and then stir.

3. Heat for up to another 30 seconds, and then stir again.
4. Add the pureed pear and milk to taste.

Sweetened Porridge for One

Serves 1

⅓ cup rolled oats
⅔ cup cold water
1 tsp pure maple syrup
Milk to taste

1. Place oats and water into a microwave-safe bowl.
2. Cook in the microwave on HIGH (100%) for 1 minute, and then stir.
3. Heat for up to another 30 seconds.
4. Stir through the syrup.
5. Add milk to taste.

Caution:

Do not leave the porridge unattended while cooking as it may overflow if heated for too long.

Dips and Soups

Bean Dip
Chicken Stock
Cream of Celery Soup
Hearty Winter Soup
Lettuce Soup
Pea and Ham Soup
Warm Cheesy Dip

Bean Dip

Approximately 300g (10oz) of 3 bean mix
½ tsp garlic – minced
½ tsp malt vinegar
Pinch of salt

1. Puree all ingredients together.
2. Refrigerate for at least 1 hour before serving with a selection of celery sticks, green beans or Pita Crisps (see recipe in the 'Dough, Pastries and Batters' section) or rice crackers.

Chicken Stock

This recipe makes approximately 2L (roughly 2 quarts) of stock, and is also suitable for a pressure cooker or slow cooker. (For pressure cookers and slow cookers, adjust the cooking times according to the manufacturer's instructions.)

2 chicken frames – rinsed
1 celery stalk with the leaves
⅓ leek – whole
1-2 sprigs of parsley
2-3L (approximately 2-3 quarts) cold water, as needed
Pinch of salt

1. Place rinsed chicken frames in a large, deep saucepan and cover with the water.
2. Add the remaining ingredients to the pot and turn to high heat on the stovetop.
3. When it reaches boiling point, reduce to a simmer and cover, cooking gently for 2-3 hours.
4. Strain the stock and place into a large bowl or jug to cool overnight in the refrigerator.

5. Remove any layer of fat from the top of the stock before use.

Tips:

Stock can be frozen in ice-cube trays or larger portions. For best results, allow the stock to reduce by half by boiling it uncovered. Ice cube-sized frozen stock can then easily be dissolved in boiling water or melted in the microwave.

Stock can also be made with chicken bones from a cooked chicken. Remove all the cooked skin, and rinse the carcass out to remove all traces of stuffing. Many people may not know that cooked chickens from stores usually have stuffing, which often includes onion.

Cream of Celery Soup

Serves 4-6

4 tsp sunflower oil
2 tsp butter
1 leek – sliced
1 shallot (green onion / spring onion / scallion / bunching onion) – diced
2 tsp minced garlic
3-4 stalks of celery – diced
2-2½ cups chicken stock – see recipe above in this section
⅓ cup gelatin-free very thick cream (in Australia, 'double cream'; in North America, 'heavy cream')
Salt – to taste
Chives – chopped for garnishing

1. Heat the oil and the butter in a large saucepan, over medium heat.
2. Add the leek and garlic, and fry gently for 2-3 minutes.

3. Add the celery and fry until the celery softens (about 1-2 minutes).
4. Pour the stock into the pan, add a pinch of salt and reduce the pan to simmer until the celery is tender (about 10-15 minutes).
5. Remove from the heat and add the cream.
6. Using a stick blender or liquidiser, blend the soup until it has a smooth, pureed consistency.
7. Serve hot and garnished with chopped chives.

Tip:

For a lactose-free version, try replacing butter with the fat skimmed from the top of the stock and some additional oil, and try using lactose-free cream.

Hearty Winter Soup

This recipe uses a slow cooker, although it could also be prepared in a pressure cooker or stove top by adjusting the cooking times (according to the manufacturer's instructions).

Serves 4-6

½ cup green split peas
½ cup yellow split peas
1 cup red lentils
*3 bacon bones **or** 1 meaty bacon hock*
5L (approximately 5 quarts) water
½ cup pearl barley
2-3 stalks celery – diced
1 leek – sliced and halved

1. Rinse all peas and lentils well.
2. Place the bacon bones into the slow cooker.

3. Cover with the water and then add the remaining ingredients.
4. Stir and cover the pot with the lid.
5. For faster cooking, set cooker to HIGH and cook for approximately 5 hours, and then reduce the cooker to LOW setting until you are ready to serve. For slower cooking, set cooker to LOW and cook 8-10 hrs.
6. Remove meat from the bones and return cut meat to the pot, mixing through.
7. Serve while hot.

Tip:

Suitable for freezing.

Lettuce Soup

Serves 4-6

4 tsp butter
½ cup leek – diced
8 tsp plain flour
1¼ cups milk
2 cups Chicken Stock – see recipe above in this section
250g (9oz) lettuce leaves including outer leaves – chopped
*¼ tsp sugar **or** a natural, calorie-free alternative*
Chopped chives for garnishing

1. Gently fry leek in butter (or use microwave at MEDIUM-HIGH setting for 2 mins) in a large saucepan.
2. Add flour and mix together.
3. Slowly add the milk, combining with the flour and leek mixture until all the milk is in the pan and no lumps are formed.
4. Add the stock, lettuce and sugar and mix well.

5. Bring to the boil and then reduce to simmer for approximately 15 minutes. Lettuce should be well wilted and the mixture hot.
6. Puree in a blender while hot.
7. Serve hot, garnished with chopped chives.

Tip:

Lettuce soup is not suitable for freezing.

Pea and Ham Soup

Serves 4-6

1 cup split peas
2L (approximately 2 quarts) water
½ cup red lentils
2-3 bacon bones
4 tsp thickened, gelatin-free cream

1. Prepare peas by soaking in 2 cups of water for approximately 1 hour, then rinse and drain.
2. Place all ingredients into a large pot and bring to the boil uncovered.
3. Scoop the foam from the top of the liquid and then cover and simmer for a further 2-3 hours.
4. Remove the meat from the bones and return the meat to the pot.
5. Add the thickened gelatin-free cream to taste.
6. Blend until at a pureed consistency.
7. Serve while hot.

Tip:

This recipe is also suitable for pressure cooking after removing the foam.

Warm Cheesy Dip

Approximately 1 litre (1 quart) of white sauce – see recipe in the 'Spreads, Sauces & Condiments' section
1½ cups cheese – grated
2 shallots (green onions / spring onions / scallions / bunching onions) – white part, diced
*½ - 1 cup cubed ham **or** diced cooked bacon*

1. Add all ingredients to the hot white sauce, stirring well until the cheese has melted.
2. Pour the dip into a serving bowl.
3. Serve warm with a selection of dippers – for example, celery sticks, fresh beans with the ends trimmed, or homemade pita crisps (see recipe in the 'Dough, Pastries and Batters' section).

Dough, Pastries and Batters

Cheesy Soda Bread

This bread is best served warm.

Serves 4

2 cups self-raising flour
1 tsp cream of tartar
1 tsp bicarbonate soda
⅔ cup milk
6 tsp sunflower or canola oil
Pinch of salt
1 cup cheese – grated

1. Pre-heat oven to 230°C/440°F.
2. In a mixer or a large mixing bowl, place the flour, cream of tartar and salt, and mix together.
3. In a separate container, dissolve the bicarbonate soda in the milk and then add the oil to this mixture.
4. Add this mixture to the mixing bowl, and mix together.
5. Add the cheese, and mix thoroughly.
6. Knead lightly and form into a loaf. (You could use an automatic mixer with a dough hook.)
7. Place in a prepared or lined loaf pan and bake at 230°C/440°F for 10-15 minutes.
8. Reduce heat to 200°C/390°F and cook a further 10-15 minutes, or until it looks cooked. Remember that a cooked bread sounds hollow when tapped on the top.

Corn Fritters

These are a great substitute for take-away or an easy Sunday night dinner.

Serves 4

1 cup self-raising flour
1 cup plain flour
¼ cup sunflower or canola oil
2 tsp baking powder – see recipe in the 'Baking' section
1 cup milk
420g (19oz) creamed corn

Butter

1. Mix/beat all ingredients together until there are no lumps.
2. Heat frypan to approximately 180°C/350°F and wipe over the cooking surface of the frypan with butter.
3. In batches and using an ice-cream scoop, spoon mixture into the pan to form fritters and cook each one until its first side starts to bubble in the centre.
4. Turn and cook until centre springs back when lightly touched with a finger.
5. Place cooked fritters on a covered platter lined with paper towelling and cover with paper towelling to prevent them going soggy - or serve straight to waiting mouths and keep them coming!

Tip:

Use a paper towel smeared with butter and wipe over the cooking surface of the frypan.

Dough for Pizza

Makes 1 family-sized pizza base (for 2-4 people)

3 cups self-raising flour
½ tsp salt

½ tsp sugar
1½ tsp baking powder – see recipe in the 'Baking' section
1 cup water
⅓ cup sunflower or canola oil

Hand Method

1. Place flour, salt, sugar and baking powder in a mixing bowl.
2. Make a well in the centre and add the water and oil, gradually combining all the ingredients with a metal knife.
3. Knead on a floured surface for about 5-7 minutes until the dough has a smooth and elastic consistency.
4. On a floured surface, roll out the dough into an appropriate shape for the chosen tray, and place onto a pizza tray lined with non-stick baking paper.

Machine Method:

1. Place flour, salt, sugar and baking powder in a mixing bowl.
2. In an electric mixer with a dough hook, mix the ingredients about 5-7 minutes until dough has a smooth and elastic consistency.
3. On a floured surface, roll out the dough into an appropriate shape for the chosen tray, and place onto a pizza tray lined with non-stick baking paper.

Flaky Pastry

Makes 1 pie crust

1¼ cup plain flour
1 tsp baking powder – see recipe in the 'Baking' section
125g (4.5oz) butter – cut into very small cubes or grated (when the butter is firm)

½ cup milk
1 tsp malt vinegar

1. Mix flour and baking powder.
2. Mix in the butter either by hand or in a mixer.
3. In a separate jug, combine the milk and malt vinegar.
4. Gradually add the milk mixture to the flour mixture, continuing to mix until it forms a fairly stiff dough. (A machine mixer with a dough hook will save a lot of time.)
5. Roll the dough thinly on a floured surface. It is now ready for use.

Serving Suggestion:

This is the perfect pastry for my Country Chicken Pie (see recipe in the 'Chicken' section).

Flour Tortillas

Makes 12 tortillas

2 cups plain flour + extra for kneading and rolling
2 tsp baking powder – see recipe in the 'Baking' section
⅓ cup sunflower oil
1¼ cups warm water

1. Mix dry ingredients in a large mixing bowl.
2. Add the oil and mix through.
3. Add the warm water a little at a time until dough is soft and not sticky.
4. Knead the dough for a few minutes (or use a machine with a dough hook).
5. Divide the mixture into 12 and shape into balls.
6. Cover the balls and allow them to rest for at least 10 minutes.

7. Heat a fry pan to medium-to-high heat. (Too high a temperature will cook the tortillas too quickly.)

8. Roll out one ball at a time using a small rolling pin, moving out from the centre of the dough and turning it until shaped similarly to a pizza crust. (I use a child-sized wooden rolling pin, the kind found in some play kitchen sets.) The result should be only about 3 mm (⅛ inch) thick.

9. Carefully lower the rolled dough into the frypan and cook each side a few seconds before turning. They should have nice brown speckles on the tortilla - just like the bought ones.

10. Remove the cooked tortilla and keep warm in a covered casserole/baking dish or wrapped in a towel.

11. Repeat steps 8 to 10 until all portions have been cooked.

Serving Suggestion:

Serve with your favourite meat and salad, and top with garlic kebab sauce (see recipe in the 'Spreads, Sauces & Condiments' section).

Uneaten portions can be frozen (separated by sheets of freezer plastic), and defrosted for later use. I really enjoy using a tortilla at a BBQ with a pork or chicken sausage in place of a bread roll.

A tortilla can also be used as a pizza base.

Fritters

A family favourite, and an excellent way to use some leftover meats. It is easy to make and surprisingly filling. Family members and friends with no food intolerances or allergies will enjoy adding tomato sauce. For the rest of us, you cannot go passed a spoonful of home-made chutney (see either the Pear and Choko/Chayote Chutney recipe or the Mango Chutney recipe in the 'Spreads, Sauces & Condiments' section).

Serves 4

1 cup self-raising flour
1 cup plain flour
¼ cup sunflower or canola oil
2 tsp baking powder – see recipe in the 'Baking' section
2 cups milk
Butter
Optional: 1 cup shredded pre-cooked meat

1. Mix/beat all ingredients together until there are no lumps.
2. Add your favourite cooked meat.
3. Heat frypan to approximately 180°C/350°F and wipe over the cooking surface of the frypan with butter.
4. In batches and using an ice-cream scoop, spoon mixture into the pan to form fritters and cook each one until its first side starts to bubble in the centre.
5. Turn and cook until centre springs back when lightly touched with a finger.
6. Place cooked fritters on a covered platter lined with paper towelling, and cover with paper towelling to prevent them going soggy. Serve hot.

Tip:

Use a paper towel smeared with butter and wipe over the cooking surface of the frypan.

Options:

Try adding a can of creamed corn in with the other ingredients in step 1.

Pita Crisps

Flour Tortillas — see recipe in this section
Canola oil spray
Home-made garlic salt — 1:1 ratio of dried pure garlic granules and sea salt

1. Pre-heat oven to 180°C/350°F.
2. Cut tortillas into wedge-shaped pieces and place in a single layer on a lightly oiled tray.
3. Spray tortillas lightly with oil and season with garlic salt.
4. Bake for approximately 20 minutes or until crisp. If you want cheesy pita crisps, sprinkle grated parmesan cheese on them after 10 minutes of cooking, and then return the tray to the oven.
5. Allow to cool and store in an air-tight container.

Scone Dough Pie Crust

Makes 1 pie (being a base and lid)

2 cups self-raising flour
25g (1oz) butter — cut into small cubes
¾ cup milk

1. Process the butter and flour in mixer or food processor (or rub in by hand).
2. Add the milk gradually while mixing to make a soft dough. (You can correct the consistency by adding a little more flour to a wet mixture, or adding a little more milk to a dry mixture.)
3. Keeping the dough soft, knead it lightly with a dough hook or by hand on a floured board.
4. Regardless of the size of the pie tin or the number of pie tins, remember to divide the dough so you have both a base and a lid.

5. Fill with desired filling and assemble the top.
6. Vent the lid by cutting small slits made in the centre with a knife (to allow steam to escape), and brush with milk before baking.

Light Meals

Chicken Savoury Spread
Garlic Cheese Pizza Bread
Lettuce Roll-Ups
Pizza
Smoked Chicken Kebabs

Chicken Savoury Spread

This makes a great topping for rice cakes or as a filling for sandwiches. The recipe can either be served as a crunchier filling by not processing it or as a spread.

Serves 4-6

Breast meat from a cooked chicken – shredded or chopped finely
1 celery stalk – diced finely
4 tsp egg-free mayonnaise
Cashew nuts to taste – crushed

1. Remove the cooked chicken meat from the bone, and add to a mixing bowl or food processor.
2. Add the celery and cashews
3. Combine well
4. **Optional**: Process in food processor until reaches the desired consistency.
5. Add mayonnaise.

Store in the refrigerator and up to 3 days.

Garlic Cheese Pizza bread

Serves 4

1 quantity home-made pizza dough – see recipe in the 'Dough, Pastries and Batters' section
30g (1oz) butter – melted
2-3 tsp garlic – crushed
1-2 cups cheese – grated
¼ cup shallot (green onion / spring onion / scallion / bunching onion) – white part, finely diced

1. Combine melted butter and garlic together.
2. Gently spread over the pizza base using a pastry brush or spoon.
3. Top with cheese.
4. Bake in oven at 200°C/390°F until cooked (approximately 20 minutes). Sprinkle the shallot onto the pizza base after 15 minutes of cooking time.

Tip:

Leave out the cheese to make a plain garlic pizza side dish.

Lettuce Roll-Ups

Serves 2-4

2 cooked chicken breasts
4-8 fresh green beans
4 tsp Pear & Choko/Chayote Chutney **or** *Garlic Kebab Sauce / Salad Dressing – both recipes in the 'Spreads, Sauces & Condiments' section*
8 large lettuce leaves

1. Slice chicken and place in all ingredients inside the centre of a lettuce leaf.
2. Add any other favourite ingredients e.g. celery, cheese
3. Roll-up and serve cold.

Pizza

Serves 4

1 quantity home-made Dough for Pizza – see recipe in the 'Dough, Pastries and Batters' section
½ tsp garlic – crushed

Pear and Choko/Chayote Chutney [see recipe in the 'Spreads, Sauces &
Condiments' section] **or** *ricotta cheese*
2-3 cups mozzarella cheese – grated
¼ - ½ cup bacon – diced
¼ - ½ cup ham – diced
¼ cup shallot (green onion / spring onion / scallion / bunching onion) – sliced
¼ cup feta cheese – crumbled

1. On a floured surface, roll out dough into an appropriate shape and place onto a pizza tray lined with non-stick baking paper.
2. Lightly spread the minced garlic over the base.
3. **Option 1**: Lightly spread chutney over the pizza base, and then sprinkle 1 cup of mozzarella cheese over the pizza base.
   Option 2: Lightly spread ricotta cheese over the pizza base.
4. Sprinkle shallot and feta cheese evenly.
5. Sprinkle the bacon and ham evenly.
6. Sprinkle the remaining mozzarella evenly.
7. Bake in 200°C/390°F oven for about 15-20 minutes or until the cheese looks lightly browned.

Tips:

Most pizzas have a clear border around the edge of about 15mm (1/2 inch) to allow you to pick up a slice by hand.

The thicker the toppings, the longer you will need to cook the pizza. I suggest not overloading the pizza otherwise you will be forced to cook the pizza for so long that the top cheese will burn.

Using Ricotta cheese on the base is a great time-saver, as it saves a bottom layer of mozzarella cheese.

Smoked Chicken Kebabs

Serves 4

2 smoked chicken breasts – cubed into bite-sized pieces
1-2 ripe pears – peeled, cored and cubed into bite-sized pieces
1 shallot (green onion / spring onion / scallion / bunching onion) – fleshy,
white section, sliced into diagonal pieces
180g (6.25oz) haloumi cheese – cubed into bite-sized pieces

1. Pre-soak wooden kebab skewers in water to prevent them from burning during cooking.
2. Cut each of the ingredients into cubes about 2.5cm (1 inch) square.
3. Slide the ingredients on the skewers, alternating the ingredients.
4. Either warm in the oven to cook the haloumi or place on a hot BBQ plate. Cook until the haloumi is lightly browned and warm.

Serving Suggestion:

Serve with a teaspoon or two of Pear and Choko/Chayote Chutney (see recipe in the 'Spreads, Sauces & Condiments' section).

Salads and Vegetables

Fruity Smoked Chicken Salad
Lentil Burgers / Patties
Oriental Salad
Pumpkin Rissoles

Fruity Smoked Chicken Salad

Serves 4

2 ripe pears
1 stalk celery
2 smoked chicken breasts

The final presentation will determine how you prepare this dish:

As a bowl of salad

1. Peel, core and dice the pears.
2. Dice the celery.
3. Cube the smoked chicken
4. Toss together.
5. Serve immediately.

As individual plates of the salad

1. Slice each pear half vertically from the base but not all the way to the top. This allows the pear slices to be fanned out.
2. Slice the smoked chicken into strips and add to the plate.
3. Slice the celery stick into long 'straws', and add to the plate, arranging them attractively with the chicken strips.
4. Serve immediately.

Serving Suggestion:

Consider drizzling this salad with Super Salad Dressing (see recipe in the 'Spreads, Sauces & Condiments' section).

Lentil Patties (for burgers)

Makes 8-10 patties

1 cup dry lentils
8 tsp pearl barley
2½ cups water
½ tsp salt
4 tsp sunflower or canola oil
1 shallot (green onion / spring onion / scallion / bunching onion) – fleshy, white section diced
¼ cup leek – diced
1 tsp garlic – minced or crushed
4 tsp soy sauce
¾ cup quick cook rolled oats
¾ cup processed bran

1. Into a saucepan, place the rinsed lentils, barley, water and salt, and bring to the boil.
2. Lower heat and simmer until the lentils are soft and splitting, by which time the water should almost be gone. This should take about 45 minutes.
3. Drain and place into a mixing bowl.
4. Gently cook the leek, garlic, shallot, and add to the mixing bowl.
5. Grind the oats to a fine consistency in a processor or blender. Add these to the mixing bowl.
6. Add the bran and soy sauce to the mixing bowl, and mix all the ingredients together.
7. Form patties from the warm mixture.
8. Either shallow fry (1-2 minutes per side), or bake in the oven at 180°C/350°F for approximately 15 minutes (or until light brown).

Serving Suggestion:

Serve with salad or wrapped in a tortilla (see recipe in 'Dough, Pastries and Batters' section).

Oriental Salad

This recipe is inspired by the one found on the back of a packet of Chang's™ Fried Noodles.

Salad base

¼ - ½ shredded green cabbage (and a little red cabbage, if desired)
1 whole shallot (green onion / spring onion / scallion / bunching onion) – diced
1-2 sticks of celery – diced
½ packet of fried noodles
Optional: ¼ cup roasted cashews

Dressing

½ cup sunflower oil
¼ cup white sugar
¼ cup malt vinegar
4 tsp soy sauce

1. Mix the dressing ingredients, and set aside. (This can be done days before, but it must be kept in the refrigerator until serving time.)
2. Combine the cabbage, shallot and celery in a salad bowl.
3. Cashews can be used raw, or cooked lightly in a frypan or microwave. Then, crush them into smaller pieces.
4. Just before serving, add cashews, noodles and dressing and toss together. Serve immediately.

Tip:

Noodles will soften upon sitting, so only add the noodles and the dressing just before serving. Also, only a small amount of the dressing is needed, and the rest can stay refrigerated until needed next (as the vinegar will preserve the dressing).

Pumpkin Rissoles

Serves 4

2 cups pumpkin – chopped
½ - 1 cup plain flour
150g (5.3oz) bacon – diced
Rolled oats
1 whole shallot (green onion / spring onion / scallion / bunching onion) – sliced thinly

1. Boil or steam the pumpkin until soft.
2. Mash the pumpkin, and then set aside to cool.
3. Cook the bacon and shallot together. Add to the mashed pumpkin.
4. Add the flour slowly while forming the mixture into balls. You will know that you have added sufficient flour if the mixture will form a ball and remain intact.
5. Roll the rissole balls in either rolled oats to form a coating.
6. Lightly fry the rissoles until golden.
7. Serve with other steamed vegetables.

Chicken

Camembert Chicken
Chicken Stuffed with Soft Cheese
Chicken a la Nietie
Country Chicken Pie
Chicken Di-Di
Easy-bake Layered Chicken Casserole

Camembert Chicken

Serves 4

1 tsp garlic – minced
150g (5oz) bacon (approximately 4 slices/rashers) – diced
1 whole shallot (green onion / spring onion / scallion / bunching onion) – diced
Sunflower or canola oil
2-3 chicken breast fillets – sliced or cubed
1 wheel Camembert cheese – roughly chopped
*¼ cup gelatin-free cream **or** milk thickened with a little arrowroot powder*

1. Gently fry the garlic, bacon, shallot in a little oil. Then, remove and set aside.
2. Brown the chicken, adding a little salt for seasoning when the meat is sealed.
3. Return the bacon and shallot to the pan and mix together, being careful not to overcook the mixture.
4. Reduce the heat to a simmer, and add the cheese and cream.
5. Stir through until the cheese has melted and a thick sauce coats the chicken.

Serving Suggestion:

Serve with rice or any vegetables which are low in salicylate (for example, cabbage, green beans, green peas, choko/chayote/mirliton/christophene).

Tips:

Brie can be substituted for Camembert cheese.

For a creamier result, remove the rind from the wheel of cheese.

Chicken a la Nietie

My version of Chicken á la King - renamed by my family using my nick-name.

Serves 6

50g (1.8oz) butter
¼ cup plain flour
1¼ cups home-made Cream of Celery Soup – see recipe in the 'Dips and Soups' section
1¼ cups milk
1-2 cups cooked chicken – shredded or diced
½ cup peas **or** *beans – cooked*

1. In a microwave-safe, casserole dish, melt the butter (at MEDIUM-HIGH for approximately 1 minute).
2. Add the flour and mix well to make a roux.
3. Microwave on HIGH (100%) for 1 minute until the roux becomes slightly powdery.
4. Pour soup into the bowl, and mix well.
5. Gradually add milk to mixture while stirring.
6. Cook for a further 4 mins on HIGH (in the microwave), stirring every 1-2 minutes.
7. Add remaining ingredients and cook on HIGH for a further 4 minutes.

Tips:

You can substitute the home-made soup with 1 cup of gelatin-free very thick cream, plus ½ cup of chicken stock (see recipe in the 'Dips and Soups' section). Some commercially-available chicken soups might be safe; however, readers are urged to check the ingredients carefully, especially for onion.

Serving Suggestion:

Serve with rice, egg-free pasta (see recipe in the 'Pasta and Rice' section), cous cous or vegetables. Great to take along to a pot-luck dinner. The only downside when I do this - there are never any leftovers to bring home.

Chicken Di-Di

My mother-in-law (Di) came up with this dish for a birthday celebration, hence the name for the recipe. She used a half cup of white wine but white rum is lower in salicylate. So, I have made the substitution here and adjusted the amount for taste, although alcohol in this recipe is optional. I suggest you only add the avocado on days you can cope with a higher level of salicylate.

Serves 4-6

¼ cup cashews
1 cup pumpkin – finely sliced
750g (26oz) chicken breast fillet
1 shallot (green onion / spring onion / scallion / bunching onion) – diced
100g (3.5oz) gelatin-free, Greek yoghurt
1 tsp garlic
100g (3.5oz) feta cheese
*Arrowroot **or** Tapioca flour*
Optional: 1 avocado (contains salicylate) – sliced
Optional: ¼ cup white rum

1. Roast the cashews lightly in the oven.
2. Fry the pumpkin until cooked and set aside.
3. Fry the garlic and chicken until chicken is cooked.
4. Add the shallot and white rum.
5. Cover and simmer 5 minutes.

6. Add the avocado, cashews, Greek yoghurt, feta cheese and cooked pumpkin.
7. Simmer uncovered a further 5 minutes allowing the pumpkin to reheat and the mixture to thicken slightly.
8. Thicken with a little arrowroot or tapioca flour blended with water.

Serving Suggestion:

Serve on a bed of rice.

Chicken Stuffed with Soft Cheese

Serves 4

125g (4.5oz) wheel of Brie cheese
½ cup gelatin-free plain or Greek-style yoghurt
*¼ tsp dried garlic granules **or** ½ tsp minced garlic*
2-3 large chicken breast fillets
150g (5oz) bacon (approximately 4 slices/rashers) – diced
Fresh parsley and chives to taste

1. Pre-heat the oven 180°C/350°F.
2. Cut the chicken fillets through the middle to make them thinner.
3. Flatten chicken slices with a meat mallet.
4. Mix together the remaining ingredients in a bowl.
5. Place 1-2 tablespoons of the mixture into the centre of each chicken fillet and roll up, folding in the sides so that no mixture is visible.
6. Wrap each rolled fillet length-wise with a bacon slice/rasher, and secure with a toothpick.
7. Bake until cooked through.

Serving Suggestion:

Serve with rice or any vegetables which are low in salicylate (for example, cabbage, green beans, green peas, choko/chayote/mirliton/christophene).

Make mini versions of the roll-ups, and place on a platter for finger food.

Country Chicken Pie

This pie is sure to surprise and delight even the fussiest of eaters. I found a way to encourage my children to start eating cabbage and celery. The pies can be made as single serves or as a family size serve, and they freeze really well. They are very handy for those times when you need something safe to eat.

Serves 4-6

750g (26oz) chicken breast fillets
1 tsp garlic – minced or crushed
Pinch of salt
150g (5oz) bacon – diced
Sunflower or canola oil
1 cup fresh green beans – trimmed
3-4 stalks of celery – diced
1 whole shallot (green onion / spring onion / scallion / bunching onion) – chopped
2 cups green cabbage – shredded
¼ cup plain flour
2 cups water
4 tsp milk
One quantity of flaky pastry as produced in the recipe in the 'Pasta and Rice' section

1. Pre-heat oven to 200°C/390°F.
2. In a large saucepan or frypan on medium high heat, brown the chicken. Add the garlic and salt when the chicken is sealed.
3. Add the bacon to the pan and fry until cooked.
4. Add the beans, celery and shallot, and fry until slightly softened.
5. Add the cabbage and stir through.
6. Once the cabbage has wilted, add the flour and mix to coat the mixture. Then add water and milk, and stir through. Allow it to simmer while you make the pastry.
7. Line an oiled pie dish with flaky pastry, and cover with some of the chicken filling.
8. Top this with a lid of pastry, sealing the sides, and then trimming off the excess. Add a few small knife cuts in the lid to allow the steam to vent when it is cooked. This prevents the final result being soggy.
9. Continue making up the pies until you run out of either filling or pastry.

Bake each pie for approximately 20 minutes or until the pastry is cooked and lightly browned.

Easy-bake Layered Chicken Casserole

Takes minutes to assemble and even less to eat!

Serves 4-6

6 chicken breast fillets or equivalent thigh fillets
4-6 slices shortcut bacon
3-4 slices of Masdaam, Jarlsburg or Swiss cheese
1⅔ cups home-made Cream of Celery Soup – see recipe in the 'Dips and Soups' section

1. Pre-heat oven to 180°C/350°F.
2. Grease an oven-proof casserole dish.
3. Line the bottom of the dish with two of the chicken fillets.
4. Cover with short-cut bacon and then add sliced cheese to the top.
5. Repeat until all chicken, bacon and cheese is used.
6. Cover the assembled casserole with the soup.
7. Bake for approximately 1 hour or until chicken is cooked through and still tender.

Serving Suggestion:

This dish is wonderful served with egg-free commercial or homemade pasta (see recipe in the 'Pasta and Rice' section).

Pork

Chinese Pork with Rice Noodles
Gyoza (Pork Dumplings)
Marinated Pork Ribs
Oriental-style Pork Meatballs
Pork Chow Mein
Pork Meatballs
Pork Sausage Casserole
Pork with Creamy Pasta

Chinese Pork with Rice Noodles

Serves 4

500g (17.5oz) pork mince
4 tsp oil
Garlic salt to taste
2-3 stalks celery – Julienned
1 whole shallot (green onion / spring onion / scallion / bunching onion) – sliced
1 cup bean sprouts
2-3 cups cabbage – shredded
1-2 sticks rice vermicelli noodles – pre-soaked in boiling water

1. Fry mince in a little oil, until cooked.
2. Season the meat with garlic salt.
3. Add celery and shallot, frying until the celery softens.
4. Add bean sprouts and cabbage.
5. If the pan is dry, add a little water or soya sauce so the vegetables can steam a little.
6. Add rice noodles. You can either stir them through the meat, or serve them on the side.

Variation:

Instead of Rice Vermicelli, add ½ packet of fried noodles and stir through, cooking until softened.

Gyoza (Pork Dumplings)

Makes 44

2 packets dumpling pastry rounds (made from flour, salt and water) available from many Asian grocery stores
500g (17.5oz) pork mince

1 whole shallot (green onion / spring onion / scallion / bunching onion) – diced
1 tsp garlic – minced
Water – for sealing dumplings
Optional: 1 tsp minced ginger (contains salicylate)

1. Mix the following together in either a bowl or a food processor: pork mince, shallot and garlic (and the optional ginger, if you are adding it).
2. Lay out the dumpling rounds on a bench/board.
3. Place a teaspoon of the mince mixture into the centre of each round.
4. To assemble each gyoza dumpling, dampen the edges with just a little water and then lay it in your palm with the mince side up. Pinch the end together, and then form two to three pleats ensuring the top is sealed.
5. Steam dumplings for 8-10 minutes or until cooked through and the pastry has softened.
6. Serve with your chosen condiment.

Marinated Pork Ribs

Serves 4

¼ cup pure maple syrup
¼ cup soy sauce
2 tsp garlic – minced
2 large pork ribs
Optional: ¼ tsp fish sauce – readers with shellfish allergies are urged to check the ingredients

1. Combine all ingredients in a jug or bowl.
2. Place the ribs in a marinade dish.
3. Pour the marinade over the ribs.

For speedy marinating, rub the marinade into both sides of the ribs.

4. Cover the meat and marinade, and refrigerate for at least an hour (or even overnight).
5. Remove ribs from the marinade, and bake, grill, fry or barbeque until cooked through.

Tip:

You can bring the marinade to the boil and thicken with a little arrowroot or tapioca flour with water (½ to 1 tsp), and serve as a dipping sauce.

Oriental-style Pork Meatballs

My children nick-named these meatballs "Hairy Pork Balls" due to the vermicelli. Whatever name you choose, I am sure you will love them.

Serves 4-6 (as a main meal)

1kg (35oz) minced pork
2 tsp garlic – crushed or minced
8 tsp pear chutney – see recipe in the 'Spreads, Sauces and Condiments' section
1 tsp soy sauce
1 cup cooked rice vermicelli – chopped

1. Soak the vermicelli in boiling water for 5 minutes. Cool in cold water, and then drain. Chop with clean scissors or a knife into smaller lengths.
2. Pre-heat oven to 180°C/350°F.
3. Mix all ingredients together in a bowl.
4. Roll approximately 1 tablespoon of the mixture into balls, and place them onto a tray lined with non-stick baking paper.
5. Repeat with remaining mixture.
6. Cook for approximately 30 minutes.

Serving Suggestion:

Serve with more vermicelli, pear chutney (see recipe in the 'Spreads, Sauces and Condiments' section) and vegetables of choice. Also great with soya sauce, cabbage and green beans.

Pork Chow Mein

Serves 4

550g (19.5oz) pork mince
8 tsp soy sauce
¼ cup pear syrup (commonly from canned pears)
1 cup green beans – frozen or fresh
1 celery stalk – cut into short straws
1-2 cups cabbage – shredded
4 tsp chives – chopped
½ packet fried noodles
¼ cup raw cashews
Optional: 2-3 sprigs of fresh coriander leaves

1. In a heated wok, stir fry the pork mince.
2. When browned, add the soy sauce and syrup and mix through.
3. Add the beans, celery and cabbage, and stir fry until the cabbage has wilted.
4. Add some fried noodles to the pan and allow to soften.
5. Stir through the chives.
6. Serve topped with fried noodles, cashews and optional coriander for garnishing.

Pork Meatballs

Serves 4-6

1kg (35oz) minced pork
4 breakfast wheat-biscuits (for example, Weetbix®/Weetabix®) – crushed
1 tsp garlic – minced
8 tsp pear chutney – see recipe in the 'Spreads, Sauces and Condiments"
section
¼ tsp salt
¼ cup grated cheese

1. Pre-heat oven to approximately 180°C/350°F.
2. Mix all ingredients together in a bowl.
3. Roll approximately 1 tablespoon of the mixture into balls, and place them onto a tray lined with non-stick baking paper.
4. Lightly spray with a suitable safe oil (for example, canola oil).
5. Cook for approximately 15 minutes or until lightly browned, turning the meatballs after about 8 minutes.

Pork Sausage Casserole

Serves 4

6-8 pork sausages
⅓ leek – chopped
¼ cup plain flour
2¼ cups water
*1 cup left-over cooked vegetables **or** fresh green beans – chopped*

1. Fry sausages until cooked.
2. Remove from pan and slice into bite-sized pieces.
3. Return sausage pieces to the pan, and add the leek to cook lightly.
4. Add the flour and stir through to coat the sausage.
5. Gradually add the water half a cup at a time stirring well, and allow the mixture to thicken between each half cup.
6. Add the vegetables.

Serving Suggestion:

Serve with cooked long grain rice.

Pork with Creamy Pasta

Serves 4

*200g (7oz) pasta – either commercial egg-free **or** home made to make 4 cups cooked pasta*
Pork leg steaks to suit number of people
200g (7oz) bacon – diced
*Fleshy, white portion of 1 leek **or** 1 whole shallot (green onion / spring onion / scallion / bunching onion)s – diced*
2¼ cups gelatin-free, light cream
3-4 tsp arrowroot
2 tsp water
Parsley or chives for garnishing

1. Boil pasta according to directions on the packet. If you are making home-made pasta, boil in 2L (8 cups) water for 3-5 minutes.
2. Grill the steaks, remove and slice into bite-sized pieces and keep warm.
3. Fry the bacon and leek (or shallot) until bacon is cooked.
4. Add the cream, and bring to the boil.
5. Simmer and add a blend of arrowroot and water to thicken the sauce.
6. Continue simmering until thickened.
7. Combine cooked pasta and the warm pork pieces in a large serving bowl, and pour hot sauce over it and mix through.

Lamb

Devilled Lamb Chops
Feta Mince with Risoni
Lamb Meatballs
Lamb Mince Casserole

Devilled Lamb Chops

Serves 4

4 lamb chump chops

Sauce

8 tsp pear chutney – see recipe in the 'Spreads, Sauces and Condiments' section
4 tsp brown sugar
2 tsp soy sauce
1 tsp malt vinegar

1. Remove all fat from the chops.
2. Combine all sauce ingredients in a jug/bowl.
3. Place chops in a single layer in a microwave-safe dish.
4. Pour the sauce over the raw meat.
5. Cook uncovered on MEDIUM-HIGH for approximately 5 minutes, or until tender and lightly brown.
6. Serve with vegetables of choice.

Tip:

Also suitable for pan frying.

Feta Mince with Risoni

Serves 4

Rice bran oil, Sunflower or Canola oil
500g (17.5oz) lamb or pork mince
1 tsp garlic – crushed or minced
1 cup fresh green beans – washed, trimmed and chopped
*Up to 8 tsp arrowroot **or** plain flour*

¼ cup water
90g (3oz) fresh feta cheese – crumbled or cubed
*1-2 cups cooked egg-free Risoni **or** some other egg-free pasta – see recipe on*
'Pasta and Rice' section
Pinch of salt

1. In a frypan (seasoned with oil), fry mince and garlic until browned.
2. Add chopped beans.
3. Coat with arrowroot or flour, and stir through.
4. Add a little of the water and stir until the mixture thickens like a sauce.
5. Add the feta cheese and reduce heat to a simmer.
6. Add the remaining water and stir until thickened.
7. Add the pasta, and stir through until coated.

Lamb Meatballs

Serves 4-6

800g (28oz) lamb mince
⅓ cup rolled oats
2 tsp garlic – crushed or minced
8 tsp pear chutney – see recipe in the 'Spreads, Sauces and Condiments'
section
4 tsp soy sauce

1. Pre-heat oven to 180°C/350°F.
2. Mix all ingredients together in a bowl.
3. Roll approximately 1 tablespoon of the mixture into balls, and place them onto a tray lined with non-stick baking paper.
4. Cook for approximately 30 minutes, turning only once during cooking.

Tip:

Meatballs should be browned and firm.

Lamb Mince Casserole

This is a super-quick dinner for the busy cook. It goes well with leftover cooked peas, fresh beans, choko/chayote/mirliton/christophene, and it is easy to add other vegetables for the rest of the family. Also, you can add some leftover cooked rice directly to the pan and stir through, heating until warmed.

Serves 4

1-2 tsp Sunflower or canola oil for frying
¾ cup leek – chopped
2 tsp garlic – minced
500g (17.5oz) lamb mince
8 tsp plain flour
1½ cups water
4 tsp pear chutney – see recipe in the 'Spreads, Sauces and Condiments'
section
2 cups rice – cooked

1. Pre-heat a frypan pan to approximately 130°C/260°F.
2. Lightly fry the leek and garlic in oil.
3. Add the lamb mince, and fry until cooked through.
4. Add the plain flour to the pan, and stir through to coat the meat.
5. Add water to the mixture ½ cup at a time and stir through, allowing to thicken before adding more water.
6. Add the chutney, and reduce to simmer when ½ cup water remains.

7. Check on the mince and stir periodically, adding 4 teaspoons of water at a time when the water in the pan has been absorbed. Aim for a gravy-like sauce texture to coat the mince.
8. Add rice, and mix through or serve on the rice

Tip:

Next time you cook rice, do a little extra for freezing in a storage bag so you can have it ready to add to casseroles or meatballs when needed. Rice can easily be defrosted in the microwave, but remember to add 1 tsp of water during defrosting to prevent it drying out. Alternatively, defrost the frozen rice in a pan of boiling water on the stove or just defrost it overnight in the refrigerator.

Pasta and Rice

Chicken Lasagne

Serves 6-8

Up to 8 tsp sunflower or canola oil
1-2 shallots (green onions / spring onions / scallions / bunching onions) – chopped
4 tsp garlic – minced
750g (26oz) chicken mince
*¼ cup plain flour **or** arrowroot*
1-2 cups home-made Cream of Celery Soup – see recipe in the 'Dips and Soups' section
2 cups milk
3 cups grated cheese
1 batch of homemade Lasagne sheets – see recipe in the 'Pasta and Rice' section
Pinch of salt

1. Oil a lasagne dish and pre-heat oven to 200°C/390°F.
2. Gently fry shallot, garlic and salt in a frypan in oil.
3. Add chicken mince, and fry until brown.
4. Reduce heat and add flour. Stir through until the mixture is coated.
5. Add the soup and 1 cup of milk, stirring through.
6. Simmer until liquid is absorbed, and then add the remainder of the milk.
7. Simmer until the mixture thickens, and then stir through 1 cup of grated cheese.
8. Place some of the chicken mixture on the bottom of the dish and then follow it with a layer of pasta sheet. Continue alternating the chicken mixture with pasta sheets, finishing with a layer of pasta.
9. Top with the 2 remaining cups of grated cheese, and bake for 30-40 minutes or until the top layer of pasta is nicely browned.

Tip:

You can substitute the cream of celery soup with an approximately 410g/14.5oz tin of condensed celery soup (if the soup's ingredients are safe for you).

Creamy Pasta Sauce

For those days when you can treat yourself to a little salicylate, this pasta sauce is delicious.

Sunflower or canola oil
1 leek – diced
1 stalk of celery – diced
1 shallot (green onion / spring onion / scallion / bunching onion) – sliced
1-2 cups pumpkin – cooked and mashed
8 tsp gelatin-free very thick cream (in Australia, 'double cream'; in North America, 'heavy cream')
2 cups homemade pasta – see recipe in the 'Pasta and Rice' section
Chopped chives or parsley as garnish
*Optional: 1 pork steak **or** ½ chicken breast fillet per person*

1. In a fry pan on medium heat, fry the leek, celery and shallot in oil.
2. Optional: add uncooked meat and cook until browned.
3. Remove this mixture from the pan, and reduce the heat.
4. Add the mashed pumpkin and the cream to pan, and stir well.
5. Return the mixture from step 3 to the pan, and simmer for approximately 10-15 minutes.
6. Add your favourite cooked egg-free pasta (see recipe in the 'Pasta and Rice' section).
7. Serve on plates, and garnish with chopped chives or parsley.

Tip:

You can substitute or complement the optional meat with any vegetables of choice.

Homemade Lasagne Sheets

Once you have tried your own fresh lasagne sheets, you'll never want to go back to the commercial dry pasta sheets. Furthermore, I find that I don't need to let the pasta rest.

3 cups fine semolina flour
1 cup warm water
½ tsp salt

1. In a mixing bowl or electric mixer, place the semolina, salt and half of the water, and mix well.
2. Gradually add the rest of the water until a stiff dough ball starts to form. (If you add too much water, simply add a little more flour until you achieve the desired consistency.)
3. Turn onto a floured surface and knead lightly so the dough is not sticky.
4. Follow the manufacturer's instructions for a pasta machine and roll through, slowly decreasing the thickness of the resulting pasta sheet with each pass through the machine.
5. Place the rolled pasta on a clean tea towel / dish towel as you go. There is no need to cover it.

Tip:

Unused pasta sheets can be frozen between sheets of freezer plastic (and then in a freezer-safe bag or container) ready for next time.

Egg-less homemade pasta

Serves 4-6

2 cups fine semolina flour
½ cup warm water
½ tsp salt

Traditional Method

1. In a large mixing bowl, mix together the semolina and the salt.
2. Add the warm water and mix to make a stiff dough, adding a little more water if the dough seems dry.
3. Turn onto a lightly floured surface and knead for 10 minutes (or knead using a dough hook in a dough-mixer).
4. Cover with plastic wrap and allow the dough to rest for 20 minutes.
5. Divide the dough into 4 segments.
6. Working with one piece at a time (while keeping the remainder covered), roll out the segment of dough very thinly and form the pasta into desired shapes.
7. Set the rolled pasta aside, and also keep it covered to avoid it drying out.
8. Cook in boiling salted water for 3 to 5 minutes, and then drain well.

Faster Method

1. Follow steps 1 to 3 above.
2. Turn onto a lightly floured surface, and give the dough a light knead.
3. Roll and shape using a pasta machine (or using some other desired method).
4. Cook in boiling salted water for 3 to 5 minutes, and then drain well.

Tip:

A pasta roller is a great help with this, as you can roll and then cut the pasta so easily.

Leftover pasta scraps can be frozen flat between sheets of freezer plastic for later use.

Pumpkin and Ricotta Cannelloni

Serves 4

2 cups pumpkin – cooked
1½ cups Ricotta cheese
1 batch of home-made eggless lasagne sheets – cut into rectangles 10cm x 13cm (4" x 5") each
1 batch of white sauce – see recipe in the 'Spreads, Sauces and Condiments' section
Lasagne dish

1. Pre-heat oven to 180°C/350°F.
2. Pre-boil the pasta sheets in boiling salted water (but do not fully cook), then drain, separate and set aside for later use. Make sure the pasta sheets do not overlap.
3. Prepare the white sauce.
4. Cover the bottom of a large rectangular baking dish with some of the white sauce.
5. Mix all the filling ingredients together.
6. Spoon this mixture generously along one of the shorter edges of the pasta sheet.
7. Gently roll the pasta sheet to form a roll with the ingredients in the middle.
8. Place the roll into the bottom of the baking dish. Make sure the seam of the pasta roll is facing down in the white sauce base.

9. Repeat steps 5-8 until all the mixture and pasta is used or until the tray is full. (It is fine for the rolls to touch each other.)
10. Cover with the remaining white sauce, and top with grated cheese.
11. Bake for 20 minutes.

Risotto - Bacon (Rice cooker version)

Serves 4

2 cups Arborio rice – uncooked
3 cups Chicken Stock – see recipe in the 'Dips and Soups' section
½ cup bacon pieces – diced
¼ cup frozen peas
Optional: ½ cup diced leek

1. Place all ingredients in the rice cooker, mix well and press start.

Risotto - Bacon (Traditional version)

Serves 4

Sunflower or canola oil
1 cup bacon – diced
*1 cup leek **or** 1 shallot (green onion / spring onion / scallion / bunching onion) – diced*
1 tsp garlic – minced
2 cups Arborio rice – uncooked
4 cups homemade Chicken Stock – see recipe in the 'Dips and Soups' section
¼ cup peas – cooked
Large saucepan

1. Fry bacon, leek and garlic in oil until cooked and lightly browned.

2. Add the uncooked rice, and stir until it is fully coated and warmed.
3. Add the chicken stock one soup ladle at a time, and stir until the liquid is absorbed before adding the next ladle of stock.
4. Keep adding the stock until all the stock is used up and the rice is cooked. (Make sure the rice is not too soggy though.)
5. Add the cooked peas and stir through.
6. Serve immediately.

Risotto - Chicken

Serves 4

Sunflower or canola oil
400g (14.5oz) chicken mince
*1 cup leek **or** 1 shallot (green onion / spring onion / scallion / bunching onion) – diced*
2-3 stalks of celery – diced
1 tsp garlic – minced
2 cups Arborio rice – uncooked
4 cups homemade Chicken Stock – see recipe in the 'Dips and Soups' section
¼ cup peas – cooked
Large saucepan

1. Fry the chicken mince, leek, celery and garlic in oil until mince is cooked.
2. Add the uncooked rice, and stir until fully coated.
3. Fry for another few minutes.
4. Add the chicken stock one soup ladle at a time, and stir until the liquid is absorbed before adding the next ladle of stock.
5. Keep adding the stock in this way until all the stock is used up and the rice is cooked. Make sure the rice is not too soggy though.
6. Add the cooked peas and stir through before serving immediately.

Fish and Seafood

Garlic Prawns
Tuna Pasta Bake
Tuna Pie

Garlic Prawns

Only make this dish for people without shellfish allergies.

Serves 4

1kg (35oz) green prawns
¼ cup sunflower oil
2 tsp garlic – minced
Pinch salt
Frypan or barbeque

1. Peel and de-vein prawns (removing the heads but leaving the tails intact).
2. Combine remaining ingredients in a large dish or bowl.
3. Toss the prepared prawns in the marinade to coat well.
4. Allow prawns to sit in the marinade for 10 minutes.
5. Lightly fry or BBQ until the prawn changes to a light orange colour.

Serving Suggestions:

This goes well as an entrée, canape or as a main meal on rice.

Tuna Pasta Bake

This dish has become a family favourite, and it is astonishingly easy to prepare.

Serves 4-6

*200g (7oz) small egg-free pasta **or** homemade pasta [in the 'Pasta and Rice' section] – uncooked*
425g (15oz) canned tuna – drained

1¼ cups of home-made Cream of Celery Soup – see recipe in the 'Dips and Soups' section
1¼ cups milk
1 cup grated cheese
Large casserole dish

1. Pre-heat oven to 200°C/390°F.
2. Combine all ingredients in a bowl, and mix.
3. Spoon into an oven-safe dish, and bake with the lid on for approximately 60 minutes.
4. Rest for approximately 5 minutes before serving.

Tips:

You can substitute the cream of celery soup with a can of an approximately 410g (14.5oz) condensed celery soup from the supermarket, if you can tolerate the ingredients (including corn starch). Make sure that whatever size can you choose, add the equivalent amount of milk.

Tuna Pie

This recipe came about as an experiment to create the equivalent of the humble quiche. It has become a favourite with my children - in spite of them not liking spinach. Two methods are included – one using filo pastry, the other using puff pastry.

Serves 4

½ cup cooked frozen spinach (which has less salicylate than fresh spinach)
200-230g (7-8oz) ricotta cheese
½ cup cheese – grated
425g (15oz) canned tuna in spring water – drained
1 shallot (green onion / spring onion / scallion / bunching onion) – sliced
150-175g (5.25-6.25oz) bacon– diced

*8 sheets of filo pastry **or** 2-3 sheets of preservative-free puff pastry*
Butter – melted
Medium-sized baking dish

Method 1 - Filo pastry

1. Cook frozen spinach according to directions on the box, squeezing out any excess water.
2. In a mixing bowl, combine the cheeses, spinach, tuna, shallot/green onions and bacon.
3. Line a buttered pie dish with 2 sheets of filo pastry.
4. Brush some butter over the top layer and add 2 more sheets of filo pastry.
5. Add a layer of the tuna mixture, spreading it evenly over the filo.
6. Add 4 more sheets of filo (buttering after 2 sheets).
7. Repeat steps 5-6 until either the dish is full or you have used all the filling.
8. Trim excess filo and place on top, spreading top layer with melted butter.
9. Cook for approximately 45mins in an oven set to 180°C/350°F.

Method 2 - Puff pastry

1. Cook the frozen spinach according to directions on the packet/box, squeezing out any excess water.
2. In a mixing bowl, combine the cheeses, spinach, tuna, shallot/green onions and bacon.
3. Line a buttered pie dish with a sheet of puff pastry.
4. Add a layer of the tuna mixture, spreading it evenly over the pastry.
5. Add another sheet of puff pastry.
6. Repeat steps 4-5 until either the dish is full or you have used all the filling.
7. Cook for approximately 45 mins in an oven set to 180°C/350°F.

Desserts

Chocolate Fudge
Chocolate Mousse
Jam Roly Poly
Pikelets (Savoury for Canapés)
Pikelets / Pancakes
Poached Pears
Self-saucing chocolate pudding

Chocolate Fudge

Great for gifts

200g (7oz) dark chocolate
100g (3.5oz) choc melts
*380g (13.5oz) tin of Nestle's Choc Top'n'Fill® **or** any equivalent chocolate-*
flavoured, sweetened condensed milk product used in desserts
4 tsp butter
Large microwave-safe dish or jug

1. Combine all ingredients in either a microwave-safe dish or jug, and cook on HIGH (100%) for 3mins (stirring occasionally).
2. Pour into a deep-sided baking tray lined with non-stick baking paper.
3. Refrigerate until set.
4. Cut into squares ready for serving.

Chocolate Mousse

Serves 8

2½ cups gelatin-free, thickened cream
2 tsp baking powder – see recipe in the 'Baking' section
¼ cup sunflower oil
¼ cup water
200g (7oz) dark chocolate

1. Beat the cream until a whipped texture. (Be careful not to overbeat the cream.)
2. Combine the baking powder, oil and water in a separate small bowl, and then add this to the cream and beat again until mixed thoroughly.

3. In a separate bowl, melt the chocolate slowly in a microwave on MEDIUM (50%) for 1 minute at a time, stirring and checking it regularly.
4. Add the melted chocolate to the mixture and beat through.
5. Pour into a serving bowls or individual dessert bowls and refrigerate until set.

Tip:

Sprinkle a Cadbury™ Flake® or grated chocolate over the set mousse just before serving for a delicious dessert.

Jam Roly Poly

Makes 8-10

Pastry:

250g (8.75oz) butter
2½ cups self-raising flour
¼ cup water to mix
½ cup Pear Jam/Jelly – see recipe in the 'Spreads, Sauces and Condiments' section

Sauce Ingredients

4 tsp butter
½ cup white sugar
3 cups water

Pastry Method

1. Rub butter into flour until it resembles fine crumbs
2. Slowly add enough water to make a sticky dough.
3. Roll pastry out on floured surface.

4. Spread with plenty of jam/jelly.
5. Fold pastry in half and then in half again so it is a log shape (or optionally, you can roll it), to fit your selected log tin.
6. Lay into a well-greased/lined log tin.

Sauce Method:

1. Melt and mix together all sauce ingredients.
2. Pour the sauce over the pastry and bake at 200°C/390°F for approximately 40 mins or until cooked.
3. Serve with whipped cream or ice-cream.

Pikelets (Savoury for Canapés)

Create party canapés with these pikelets. When spread with cream cheese and topped with smoked salmon or caviar, these will be sure to please.

This recipe is almost the same as the Pikelets/Pancakes recipe below. The only ingredients not needed from the Pikelets/Pancakes recipe are the white sugar and optional choc chips. The method is the same.

Serving Suggestion:

Use as a canapé base. You could spread any of the following on top of the base:

- Cream cheese and slices of smoked salmon or smoked chicken;
- Pear Chutney (see recipe in the 'Spreads, Sauces and Condiments' section) over chicken or slices of pork; or
- Cheese and Bacon Spread (see recipe in the 'Spreads, Sauces and Condiments' section).

Pikelets / Pancakes

Serves 4

100g (3.5oz) butter – melted
4 tsp baking powder – see recipe in the 'Baking' section
¼ cup sunflower oil
¼ cup water
2 cup milk
3 cups self-raising flour
½ cup white sugar
Optional: ¼ cup choc chips

1. In a large bowl, add the ingredients in the order listed above.
2. Beat lightly with a rotary beater until no lumps are visible.
3. Heat a frypan to approximately 180°C/350°F or until a drop of water "dances" around the pan.
4. For pikelets or mini pancakes, use an ice-cream scoop to measure the mixture for one pikelet and add to heated pan. For pancakes, use approximately ¼ of the mixture for one large pancake.
5. Turn the pikelet/pancake when bubbles break in the middle of it.
6. Cook the second side until the middle springs back when pressed lightly with a finger.
7. For pikelets, set them aside to cool on a wire rack. For pancakes, place onto a plate while hot and serve as desired.

Caution:

Over beating will result in a tougher pancake/pikelet. Left-over mixture can be refrigerated for a few days for later use.

Serving Suggestion for pikelets:

Spread with butter then top with your choice of pear jam and a dollop of thickened/whipped cream or golden syrup.

Serving Suggestion for pancakes:

Top with sifted icing sugar and pure maple syrup, or with your favourite topping or with lime syrup (see recipe in the 'Icings and Toppings' section).

Slimmer tip:

Reduce the sugar as follows: ¼ cup sugar, ½ teaspoon stevia powder, and ½ teaspoon vanilla.

Poached Pears

Serves 6

3 ripe pears – peeled, and cut into quarters without the core or seeds
¼ - ⅓ cup pure maple syrup
8 tsp brown sugar
½ cup water
1½ cups gelatin-free thickened cream – whipped

1. Place pears in an ovenproof dish.
2. Drizzle with half the maple syrup.
3. Sprinkle sugar over the pears.
4. Surround the pears with water (but don't pour it over the pears)
5. Bake uncovered at 180°C/350°F for approximately 30 minutes or until just soft.
6. Place the pears into dessert bowls and ladle over some of the juice from the dish.

7. In a bowl, stir the remaining maple syrup through the cream until combined. Alternatively, drizzle Mock-Maple Syrup (see recipe in the 'Icings and Toppings' section) over the pears, and serve with the whipped gelatin-free cream.

Self-saucing chocolate pudding

This easy dessert is a family favourite. Any leftovers in my household would be fought over.

Serves 6-8

60g butter
1½ cups self-raising flour
1 cup castor/caster sugar
½ cup extra castor/caster sugar
¼ cup cocoa powder
4 tsp extra cocoa powder
½ cup milk
2 tsp vanilla
1 tsp baking powder – see recipe in the 'Baking' section
6 tsp sunflower oil
6 tsp water
1¾ cup hot water (not boiling water)
Large microwave-safe casserole dish

1. Melt butter in microwave-safe dish on MEDIUM-HIGH (75%) for 1 minute or until it has fully melted.
2. Pour the melted butter into a mixing bowl, and add the sifted flour, milk, vanilla, ¼ cup cocoa powder and 1 cup of castor/ caster sugar.
3. In another small bowl, mix together the baking powder, sunflower oil and water. Add this mixture to the other mixing bowl (from step 2) and combine.

4. Pour the mixture into the microwave-safe dish.

5. Combine the extra measures of sugar and cocoa powder, and sprinkle over the top of the pudding mixture.

6. Gently add the hot water to cover the topping by pouring it onto an up-turned spoon held low over the bowl. Ideally, this should not significantly disturb the sugar and cocoa powder sprinkled on top of the dessert mix.

7. Cover and cook on HIGH (100%) for approximately 8 minutes.

8. Dust with icing sugar and serve while warm.

Tip:

Pouring the hot water onto an up-turned spoon held low over the bowl, will prevent disturbing the sugar and cocoa powder mixture.

This dessert goes really well with ice-cream or cream, which, of course, should be gelatin-free and egg-free.

Caution:

DO NOT use boiling water in step 6 as it will cause the mixture to boil over during cooking.

Baking

Apple Muffins

Makes approximately 30 mini muffins or 12 large ones.

2-3 golden delicious apples – peeled, cored and chopped
1¼ cups milk
2 tsp baking powder – see recipe in the 'Baking' section
1 tsp vanilla
50g (1.75oz) butter – chopped
4 tsp sunflower or canola oil
4 tsp gelatin-free, plain or Greek-style yoghurt
2½ cups self-raising flour
1 cup rolled oats
⅓ - ½ cup brown sugar – packed firmly

1. Pre-heat oven to 180°C/350°F.
2. Prepare muffin pans with spray-on sunflower or canola oil. (The pans could be floured instead, if preferred).
3. Except for the flour and oats, place all ingredients into a blender and process until a thick texture is achieved.
4. Place flour and oats in a large mixing bowl, and stir to combine.
5. Fold the apple mixture into the flour and oats.
6. Using an ice-cream scoop, place mixture into muffin pans.
7. Bake in the oven for approximately 15-20 minutes or until cooked.

Tip:

Muffins are cooked when the centre springs back when gently touched with a finger.

Baking powder

Did you know that most commercially available baking powders contain corn starch? It is very easy to make your own but without the corn starch.

Makes 125g (4.5oz)

4 tsp cream of tartar
4 tsp arrowroot
4 tsp bicarbonate soda

1. Sift and mix all ingredients and pour into an air-tight container.

Tips:

As long as you keep the ratio of the 3 ingredients the same, you can make whatever quantity you desire.

Larger quantities are best stored in the freezer.

Note:

An alternative baking powder in some recipe books uses 2 parts cream of tartar and 1 part bicarbonate soda.

Banana Cake

One piece of this cake will have you begging for more.

50g (1.75oz) butter
1 large ripe or over-ripe Cavendish banana
¾ cup brown sugar
8 tsp milk

1 tsp baking powder – see recipe in the 'Baking' section
6 tsp water
6 tsp sunflower or canola oil
1½ cups self-raising flour
Optional: ¼ cup chocolate bits

1. Pre-heat the oven to 180°C/350°F.
2. Except for the flour, place all the ingredients into a blender and process until pureed.
3. Sift flour into a large mixing bowl.
4. Add the blended puree to the flour and fold through.
5. Pour into a lined/greased bar tin and cook at 180°C/350°F for approximately 45mins or until an inserted skewer comes out clean.

Serving Suggestion:

Dust with icing sugar. If you have added the optional chocolate chips, ice with Butter Icing (see recipe in the 'Icings and Toppings' section).

Serve warm or cooled.

Tip:

I recommend a banana that is not high in salicylate, and so suggest avoiding Lady Finger / Sugar bananas.

Banana Muffins

Makes 12

50g (1.75oz) butter
1 large ripe or over-ripe Cavendish banana
½ cup brown sugar

8 tsp milk
1 tsp baking powder – see recipe in the 'Baking' section
½ cup milk
6 tsp sunflower or canola oil
1-1½ cups unprocessed bran
1½ cups self-raising flour

1. Pre-heat oven to 180°C/350°F.
2. Except for the flour and the bran, place all the ingredients into a blender and process until pureed.
3. Place flour and bran in a large mixing bowl, and stir to combine.
4. Add blended puree to the combined flour and bran, and fold through.
5. Spoon into muffin pans (greased or lined with muffin papers) or into smaller cupcake pans for mini muffins.
6. Bake for approximately 15-20 minutes or when the centre springs back when gently touched with a finger.

Tip:

I recommend a banana that is not high in salicylate, and so suggest avoiding Lady Finger / Sugar bananas.

Butter Cookies

The best thing about this recipe is that you can store the dough in the refrigerator and cook when needed, for example when unexpected guests drop in. The dough will store for up to 2 weeks tightly wrapped in the refrigerator.

Makes 35

100g (3.5oz) softened butter
100g (3.5oz) castor/caster sugar

4 tsp Pear Jam/Jelly – see recipe in the 'Spreads, Sauces and Condiments'
section
6 tsp milk
1 tsp vanilla
1 cup plain flour

1. Except for the flour, place all the ingredients in a large mixing bowl and beat well.
2. Stir in the flour and mix to a stiff dough, and roll into long logs. The thickness should be one cookie in diameter.
3. Wrap tightly with plastic wrap and chill in the refrigerator for approximately 8 hours or until needed.
4. When needed, cut circular slices of the dough about 6mm thick, and place on a cookie sheet.
5. Bake in oven pre-heated to 180°C/350°F for 10-12 minutes or until cooked. Alternatively, cook in a microwave oven on MEDIUM (50%) for 2½ - 3 minutes, or until just dry in the centre.
6. Cool on a wire rack.

Chocolate Brownies

Yes, it really is possible to make delicious egg-free brownies!

Makes 12

2⅓ cups plain flour
1 cup water
⅔ cup cocoa powder
125g (4.5oz) butter – melted
2 cups white sugar
1 tsp vanilla
2½ tsp baking powder – see recipe in the 'Baking' section
Pinch of salt
Pure icing sugar

1. Pre-heat oven to 180°C/350°F.
2. In a microwave-safe jug or bowl, mix ⅓ cup plain flour with the water and cook on HIGH (100%) for approximately 1½ minutes (whisking every 30 seconds) until a pasty texture is created.
3. Transfer to a large mixing bowl and set aside to cool.
4. In a jug, add the cocoa powder to the melted butter and stir to combine thoroughly. Then add this mixture to the mixing bowl.
5. Add the sugar, vanilla, baking powder, salt and the remainder of the flour to the mixing bowl.
6. Beat to combine all of the ingredients.
7. Pour into a lined slice or small lamington (deep-sided) oven tray.
8. Bake for approximately 35-45 minutes or until mixture pulls away from the side of the tray slightly. Use the skewer test - it should come out clean if inserted into the middle of the tray.
9. Cut into squares once cooled and dust with pure icing sugar to serve.

Tip:

Brownie will firm upon cooling, so be careful not to overcook. Cooking time will depend on the size of the tray used.

Chocolate Cake

This is a lovely light and fluffy chocolate cake. No-one would guess that it is egg-free!

50g (1.75oz) butter – melted
2 cups self-raising flour
4 tsp baking powder – see recipe in the 'Baking' section
½ cup sunflower oil
½ cup water
1½ cups white sugar

½ tsp vanilla
⅓ cup cocoa powder
1 cup milk

1. Pre-heat oven to 180°C/350°F.
2. Mix all ingredients together, and beat for approximately 1 minute.
3. Pour into two 20cm round cake tins lined with non-stick baking paper.
4. Cook for approximately 1 hour.
5. Allow to cool in the tin.
6. Carefully turn one cake out onto a suitable plate/container lined with non-stick baking paper, and ice the top with either chocolate icing or chocolate ganache.
7. Turn out the other cake so it sits on top of the first one.
8. Cover the combined, layered cake with more icing/ganache.

Chocolate Custard Slice

This recipe came about on Christmas Eve when I'd run out of vanilla. Very tasty!

Makes 1 tray

¼ cup plain flour
2 cups milk
¼ cup cocoa powder
8 tsp castor/caster sugar
1 tsp arrowroot, blended with a little water
1 packet of large, square cracker biscuits (Australian 'Sao'-style are great if you can tolerate yeast, or use a ready-made preservative-free, butter puff pastry)

1. In a large saucepan or a microwave-safe container, mix the flour with a little of the milk to make a paste.

2. Continue adding the milk slowly stirring out any lumps until all milk is added.

3. Add the sugar and vanilla and stir through.

4. If using the stove, gently heat the mixture and stir until sugar is dissolved and then bring to the boil. Reduce heat and stir until mixture thickens.
   If using a microwave, cook on HIGH (100%) in 30 - 60 second bursts, whisking or stirring the mixture in between cooking.

5. Remove from the heat and stir through the blended arrowroot mixture.

6. Heat for another 30 seconds in microwave or on the stove top.

7. Line the base of a slice tin with the pastry or biscuits.

8. Pour the custard over while hot.

9. Top with another layer of biscuits or pastry.

10. Cover immediately with plastic wrap and refrigerate until set.

11. Once set, mix together pure icing sugar with a little water to make a glaze icing and use to cover. If your dietary restrictions allow, add a little cocoa powder to the icing.

Chocolate Iced Weetbix® /Weetabix® Slice

Makes 1 tray

1 cup self-raising flour
½ cup brown sugar
3 breakfast wheat-biscuits (for example, Weetbix® /Weetabix®) – crushed
125g (4.5oz) butter

1. Pre-heat oven to 180°C/350°F.

2. Place all dry ingredients into a large mixing bowl and mix to combine.

3. Melt the butter and pour over the dry ingredients and mix thoroughly.

4. Spread into a slice tin and bake for approximately 15 minutes or until golden brown.
5. Mark into squares while still warm and soft
6. Ice with chocolate icing when cool.

Tip:

Slice firms upon cooling, so avoid overcooking the slice.

Chocolate Mud Cake

Just because you can't eat eggs doesn't mean you have to miss out on chocolate mud cake that would fool even the connoisseur. My family encouraged me to keep trying until I got the recipe just right.

250g (8.75oz) butter cubed
200g (7oz) dark cooking chocolate – either chopped from a block or as drops
2 cups white sugar
1 cup very strong, decaffeinated coffee
1 tsp vanilla
¼ cup white rum
¼ cup cocoa powder
1 cup self-raising flour
¾ cup plain flour

Egg Replacer ingredients – equivalent to 2 eggs:

2 tsp baking powder – see recipe in the 'Baking' section
¼ cup sunflower oil
¼ cup water

Other equipment:

Aluminium foil
Optional: 1 wet towel (see tips below)

1. Preheat oven approximately 150°C/300°F (fan-forced).
2. You will need either one deep 20cm (8") tin or two shallower 20cm (8") tins for this recipe. Line with non-stick baking paper.
3. Combine to melt the following ingredients in either a double saucepan (on the stove) or suitable dish in the microwave: butter, chocolate, sugar and the strong coffee until the chocolate is melted and a smooth mixture is formed. (I prefer to use the microwave for 1 minute on HIGH, stirring after 30 seconds.)
4. Allow to cool to lukewarm.
5. Add the vanilla and white rum.
6. Make egg substitute in a small bowl mixing the baking powder with the oil and water, and adding this to the chocolate mixture.
7. Stir through well to combine.
8. Pour the chocolate mixture into a large mixing bowl.
9. Gradually add the flours and cocoa powder, and mix until there are no lumps and the mixture is smooth.
10. Pour into tin(s), cover with aluminium foil and bake for about 2 hours.
11. Remove the foil.
12. Continue cooking until the cake passes the skewer test – that is, it comes away clean when stuck into the centre of the cake.
13. Allow to cool in the tin. Once cold, encase the cake (tin and all) in plastic wrap and put in the refrigerator overnight.
14. Cover with chocolate ganache (see recipe in the 'Icings and Toppings' section) to finish.

Tips:

Wrap a wet towel around the cake to prevent the outside from cooking faster than the middle of the cake. This towel remains around the cake while it is cooking.

The cooking time will be shorter for 2 tins than when cooking just 1 tin.

Cake firms on cooling and refrigeration.

Do not use silicon bake-ware as the cake may break when removed from the oven.

Double Chocolate Slice

Makes 1 tray

2 cups self-raising flour
1½ cups white sugar
¼ cup cocoa powder
¼ cup chocolate chips
2 tsp baking powder – see recipe in the 'Baking' section
4 breakfast wheat-biscuits (for example, Weetbix® /Weetabix®) – crushed
¼ cup water
¼ cup sunflower oil
100g (3.5oz) butter – melted

1. Pre-heat oven to 180°C/350°F.
2. Line two slice trays with non-stick baking paper, and set aside.
3. Place all dry ingredients into a large mixing bowl, and mix to combine.
4. Add the water, oil and melted butter, and mix to combine well. The mixture should clump together when squeezed. If it does not, add a little more melted butter.
5. Place the mixture into the slice trays with half in each tray, and then press into the tin.
6. Cook for approximately 15-20 minutes. Note that it won't harden until cooled, so avoid overcooking the slice.
7. Mark into squares while the slice is still warm and soft.

Dairy-Free Variation:

Use carob powder and buds in place of chocolate, and substitute butter with margarine.

Egg Replacer

Replacement for 1 egg

1 tsp baking powder
6 tsp sunflower oil
6 tsp water

1. Add all ingredients to a mixing bowl in the order listed above.
2. Whisk together, and use promptly.

Alternative

For those with no intolerance to salicylate, try mixing chia seeds with water (to supplier's instructions) to make a gel, which can be refrigerated for later use.

Golden Syrup Cakes

This is an adaptation of my Jewish great-grandmother's recipe for Honey Cakes. It was quite a challenge to find a safe substitute without the spices or honey and to be able to live up to expectations from the family. I am pleased to report that it is consumed with the same enthusiasm and speed as the traditional version.

Makes approximately 85

3 tsp baking powder – see recipe in the 'Baking' section
⅓ cup sunflower oil
⅓ cup water
2 cups white sugar
1½ cups golden syrup
1 tsp bicarbonate soda
1kg (35oz) self-raising flour (but have more on hand, in case it is needed)
Castor/caster sugar

1. Pre-heat oven 180°C/350°F.
2. In a small bowl or jug, mix the baking powder, oil and water, and whisk together.
3. Place the sugar and the whisked mixture into a large mixing bowl or machine mixing bowl.
4. Warm the golden syrup either in a microwave (MEDIUM setting – 50%) or on the stove-top.
5. Add the bicarbonate soda to the warmed syrup, and then add this to the sugar mixture and mix well.
6. Add 2 cups of sifted self-raising flour, mixing thoroughly to form a stiff dough, slowly adding more flour a little at a time.
7. If you have a machine with a dough hook, you can continue adding the flour until the mixture loses a lot of its stickiness and pulls away from the side of the bowl. Otherwise, you will need to add the flour while kneading on a floured board, working the flour into the dough.
8. Keep kneading and adding flour until the dough feels almost dry to the touch. It will seem like you have too much flour but keep kneading until all the flour is worked in.
9. Roll the mixture into small balls and dip in castor/caster sugar.
10. Place on an oven tray lined with non-stick baking paper.
11. Bake until the cakes start to look a light golden brown (approximately 12-15mins).
12. Remove from trays while still hot, and allow them to cool on a kitchen towel.
13. Once cold, pack into air-tight containers with a slice or two of fresh bread and allow the cakes to soften over a couple of days (replacing the bread as it dries).

Tips:

To test if the dough is ready to roll into balls, break a section apart. It should break cleanly and not drag when pulled into 2 pieces.

Ensure that you allow the cakes to rest a few days with the bread in place, swapping the bread as it dries out as this is key to adding moisture to the cakes. They are not meant to be eaten as rock cakes, but softening the cakes in a container with the bread will make it worth the wait.

Lime Cake

1½ cups white sugar
2 limes
125g (4.5oz) butter
½ cup milk
¼ cup water
¼ cup sunflower oil
2 cups self-raising flour
8 tsp poppy seeds

1. Pre-heat oven to 180°C/350°F.
2. Cut off the ends of each lime, allowing enough flesh in the ends for juicing. Set aside for later use in the icing.
3. Remove the peel from the remaining limes, and cut into small pieces.
4. Except for the flour and poppy seeds, place all ingredients in a blender and blend until pureed.
5. In a large electric mixing bowl, place the flour and the blended mixture and mix for 1 minute on low-to-medium speed, or hand mix until smooth and well combined.
6. Gently stir through the poppy seeds.
7. Bake for approximately 45-50 minutes or until cooked.
8. Allow to cool in the tin before icing.

Tip:

Spread Lime Glaze Icing (see recipe in the 'Icings and Toppings' section) or drizzle Mock-Maple Syrup (also in the 'Icings and Toppings' section) over the cake.

Muesli Slice

Makes 1 tray

Approximately 400g (14oz) condensed milk
2½ cups rolled oats
½ cup cashews – chopped
1 golden delicious apple or pear – peeled and chopped
Optional for those who can cope with salicylate: 100g (3.5oz) dried
*blueberries **or** dried pears*

1. Pre-heat oven to 150°C/300°F.
2. Warm the condensed milk in either a saucepan (on low heat) or in the microwave on a LOW (30%) setting.
3. Add remaining ingredients, and mix until well combined.
4. Press mixture into a greased tin.
5. Bake for 30-40mins or until top is brown.
6. Allow to cool before cutting into squares.

Tip:

As an alternative to condensed milk, try a tin of Nestle's caramel or chocolate Top'n'Fill®, a sweetened condensed milk product used in desserts, including for filling tarts.

Oaty Chocolate-Chip slice

Makes 2 trays of thin slice or 1 tray of a thicker slice. This slice is suitable for freezing.

2 cups self-raising flour
1½ cups white sugar
1 cup rolled oats
¾ - 1 cup chocolate chips
2 tsp baking powder – see recipe in the 'Baking' section
¼ cup water
¼ cup sunflower oil
100g (3.5oz) butter

1. Pre-heat oven to 180°C/350°F.
2. Line slice tray(s) with non-stick baking paper, and set aside.
3. Place all dry ingredients into a large mixing bowl, and mix to combine.
4. Combine the water, oil and melted butter, and add to dry mixture and combine well.
5. Place the mixture into the slice tray(s), and then press down gently.
6. Cook for approximately 15 minutes, or longer if you want a biscuit/cookie rather than a slice. Note that it won't harden until cooled, so avoid overcooking the slice.
7. Mark into squares while the slice is still warm and soft.

Tip:

The mixture should clump together when squeezed. If not, add a little more butter.

Poppy Seed Cake

A twist on my friend Alix's orange poppy seed cake recipe.

⅓ cup poppy seeds
½ cup plain, gelatin-free yoghurt
200g (7oz) butter
4 tsp lime rind – finely grated
1 cup white sugar
3 tsp baking powder – see recipe in the 'Baking' section
1 cup pear syrup from canned pears
⅓ cup sunflower oil
6 tsp water
1½ cups self-raising flour
½ cup plain flour

1. Pre-heat oven to 180°C/350°F.
2. Combine poppy seeds and yoghurt, and set aside to allow the poppy seeds to soften.
3. Place butter, rind and sugar into a mixing bowl, and beat with an electric mixer until creamed.
4. Add flour, baking powder, ¼ cup of the pear syrup, water and the oil, and beat well.
5. Stir through the yoghurt and poppy seed mixture and the remainder of the pear syrup, and mix gently so it is well combined.
6. Pour cake mixture into a greased or lined 20cm/8" cake tin, and bake for approximately 45-50 minutes or until cooked (as tested with a skewer).

Serving Suggestion:

Make a lime syrup (see recipe in the 'Icings and Toppings' section) to pour over warm cake and serve with a dollop of fresh cream. Alternatively, allow the cake to cool in the tin on a wire rack before turning out and covering with butter icing (see recipe in the 'Icings and Toppings' section).

Poppy Seed Muffins

Makes 12

125g (4.5oz) softened butter
2 tsp lime rind – finely grated
⅔ cup white sugar
2 tsp baking powder – see recipe in the 'Baking' section
¼ cup sunflower oil
1¼ cups milk
2 cups self-raising flour
8 tsp poppy seeds

1. Pre-heat oven to 180°C/350°F.
2. Grease or line a 12-hole muffin pan.
3. Place the butter, rind and sugar into a mixing bowl, and beat with an electric mixer until creamed.
4. Add baking powder, oil, milk and flour, and beat well.
5. Beat for a further minute or two until mixture becomes light and airy.
6. Gently stir in the poppy seeds.
7. Spoon mixture into the muffin tin and bake for approximately 20 mins.
8. Turn onto a wire rack to cool.

Pouring Custard

Makes approximately 500ml (2 cups)

8 tsp plain flour

*2 cups milk + 2 tsp vanilla **or** 2 cups vanilla soy milk*
8 tsp castor/caster sugar
Optional: yellow food colouring (if you are <u>not</u> allergic)

1. In a large saucepan or a microwave-safe container, mix the flour with a little of the milk to make a paste.
2. Continue adding the milk slowly stirring out any lumps until all the milk is added.
3. Add the castor/caster sugar and vanilla (or vanilla soy milk), and stir through.
4. If using the stove, gently heat the mixture and stir until the sugar is dissolved, and then bring to the boil. Reduce heat and stir until mixture thickens.
    If using a microwave, cook on HIGH (100%) in 30 - 60 second bursts, whisking or stirring the mixture in between cooking.
5. Remove from the heat. You could then add yellow food colouring if desired and if you are not sensitive to it.

Scones (Lemonade)

Makes 12-14, depending on the size that you desire.

4 cups self-raising flour
1¼ cups preservative-free lemonade
1¼ cups thickened, gelatin-free cream
Milk

1. Pre-heat oven to 200°C/390°F.
2. Place flour in mixing bowl.
3. Add lemonade and cream, and stir ingredients together quickly.
4. Turn out into a floured tray.
5. Cut into squares and brush tops with a little milk.
6. Bake for approximately 15-20 minutes.

Tip:

If the mixture can't be cut into squares because it is too runny, you can either thicken the mixture with a little more flour or cut it into squares after cooking.

Scones (Plain)

Makes 12-14, depending on the size that you desire.

2 cups self-raising flour
½ tsp salt
8 tsp butter – melted
¾ - 1 cup milk
Extra flour for rolling

1. Pre-heat oven to 200°C/390°F.
2. Place flour and salt in a large mixing bowl, making a well in the centre.
3. Add melted butter and milk.
4. Using a stainless-steel butter knife, mix lightly into a moist dough.
5. Turn out onto a floured board and knead very lightly. Press out to 5cm/2" thickness.
6. Cut out with a scone cutter placing close together on a lined tray.
7. Brush tops with milk.
8. Bake 12-15 minutes.
9. Wrap in a clean tea towel/dish towel or cloth until cooled.

Shortbread Biscuits

These biscuits are just one of many that the family calls "Granny Joy's biscuits". I don't remember ever visiting my grandparents without there being a selection of delicious biscuits, including these. We enjoyed them as children and now our children enjoy them also. They could arguably be called "the best shortbread biscuits ever".

Makes approximately 70

250g (8.75oz) butter
1 cup pure icing sugar – sifted
2½ cups plain flour

1. Pre-heat oven to 180°C/350°F.
2. Cream the butter and sugar together.
3. Add the flour, and mix until the pastry forms a ball.
4. Roll into small balls (about 1-2 tsp of mixture per ball), place on trays lined with non-stick baking paper and then flatten with a fork.
5. Cook until they just start to brown on the edges (approximately 15 minutes). The secret is not to overcook these biscuits.

Vanilla Slice

Inspired by my cousin Cathy's delicious vanilla slice, I gave myself the ultimate challenge of making a custard slice without egg, custard powder or corn flour. When you taste this recipe, you will never know the difference! For those not sensitive to food colouring, add a few drops of yellow food colouring to the custard mixture to give it that traditional yellow colour.

Makes 1 tray

¼ cup plain flour
2 cups milk
8 tsp castor/caster sugar
2 tsp vanilla

1 tsp arrowroot, blended with a little water
Optional: yellow food colouring (if you are <u>not</u> allergic)
1 packet of large, square cracker biscuits (Australian 'Sao'-style are great
if you can tolerate yeast, or use a ready-made preservative-free, butter puff
pastry)

1. In a large saucepan or a microwave-safe container, mix the flour with a little of the milk to make a paste.
2. Continue adding the milk slowly stirring out any lumps until all milk is added.
3. Add the sugar and vanilla, and stir through.
4. If using the stove, gently heat the mixture and stir until sugar is dissolved and then bring to the boil. Reduce heat and stir until mixture thickens.
    If using a microwave, cook on HIGH (100%) in 30 - 60 second bursts, whisking or stirring the mixture in between cooking. Continue until mixture resembles a thick custard texture (which should be approximately 5 minutes). Remove from the heat and stir through the blended arrowroot mixture.
5. Heat for another 30 seconds in either microwave or on the stove top.
6. Add yellow food colouring if desired (and if not sensitive to it).
7. Line the base of a slice tin with the pastry or biscuits.
8. Pour the custard over while hot.
9. Top with another layer of biscuits or pastry.
10. Cover immediately with plastic wrap and refrigerate until set.
11. Once set, mix together pure icing sugar with a little water to make a glaze icing, and use to cover. If your dietary restrictions allow, add a little passionfruit to the icing.

Icing and Toppings

Butter Icing

Perfect for banana cake (see recipe in the 'Baking' section).

Makes enough to cover one cake

1 cup pure icing sugar – sifted
25g (1oz) butter
4 tsp milk
½ tsp vanilla

1. Place icing sugar and butter into a small mixing bowl, and mix with a metal fork until creamed.
2. Add the milk and mix thoroughly.
3. Add the vanilla and beat thoroughly.

Tip:

To make creaming the butter and sugar easier, use butter at room temperature or alternatively grate refrigerated butter.

Chocolate Ganache

Perfect for mud cake (see recipe in the 'Baking' section).

Makes enough to cover one cake

150g (5.3oz) double, gelatin-free cream
200-250g (7.1 - 8.8oz) dark chocolate (chopped) **or** *chocolate melts*

1. Heat cream in microwave-safe jug until just boiling (see tip below).
2. Add the chocolate pieces and stir with enthusiasm (burning off some of those calories before eating them) until the chocolate is melted and the mixture thickens.

3. Onto fresh plastic wrap, invert the cake to be covered.
4. Add ganache to the cake.
5. Join 2 cakes with ganache if you are making a layered cake.

Tips:

Microwave the cream one minute at a time on HIGH (100%), stirring in between cooking. You do not want it to boil over, so stay nearby throughout the process.

You can spread the cake with pear jam to help the ganache stick securely. I've made cakes with and without the jam, and both methods work just fine.

Chocolate Icing

Makes enough to cover one cake

1½ cups pure sifted icing sugar – sifted
8-12 tsp cocoa powder
8 tsp milk

1. Combine icing sugar and cocoa powder in a small mixing bowl.
2. Gradually add the milk and stir vigorously until a spreadable texture.

Tip:

An alternative to icing sugar is a commercial icing mix using sugar and tapioca flour.

Use left-over icing to ice arrowroot biscuits as a treat for the kids. My children love icing the biscuits themselves and then licking the bowl.

Cream Cheese Frosting

Great on banana cake (see recipe in the 'Baking' section).

Makes enough to cover one cake

250g (8.8oz) preservative-free cream cheese – softened
¼ cup butter – melted
2 cups pure icing sugar – sifted
½ tsp lime juice
½ tsp vanilla

1. Beat cream cheese with melted butter.
2. Gradually add icing sugar, lime juice and vanilla. Beat until smooth.

Tip:

An alternative to icing sugar is a commercial icing mix using sugar and tapioca flour.

Lime Glaze Icing

The perfect topping for lime cake (see recipe in the 'Baking' section).

Makes enough to cover one cake

1 cup pure icing sugar – sifted
4 tsp lime juice
4 tsp water
½ tsp vanilla

1. Sift icing sugar into a small mixing bowl.
2. Add the juice and water, and mix with a metal fork until fully combined.

3. Add the vanilla and mix thoroughly.
4. If needed, add a little more water or lime juice a few drops at a time until a thin pasty consistency.

Tip:

An alternative to icing sugar is a commercial icing mix using sugar and tapioca flour.

Lime Syrup

Goes well with poppy seed cake (see recipe in the 'Baking' section) or pancakes (see recipe in the 'Breakfast Dishes' section).

Makes up to 500ml (2 cups)

2 cups white sugar
1½ cups water
1 cup fresh lime juice
½ cup lime rind – grated

1. In a saucepan, stir all ingredients over medium heat until the sugar is dissolved.
2. Simmer for approximately 15-20 minutes or until slightly thickened or like a syrup.

Serving Suggestion:

Serve hot over pancakes or over warm poppy seed cake or muffins.

Mock Cream

Makes just over ½ cup

8 tsp butter
⅓ cup castor/caster sugar
½ cup milk
½ tsp vanilla

1. Soften the butter at room temperature. (Tip: Use a grater on cold butter to speed up the process.)
2. Add the sugar, and cream the butter.
3. Very gradually, add the milk, and continue beating until no grains of sugar remain.
4. Flavour with vanilla.

Mock-Maple Syrup

Have you run out of the real thing? Don't panic, help is at hand. Try this easy 2-step recipe.

Makes approximately 1½-2 cups

1½ cups brown sugar – packed firmly
½ cup water
1½ tsp vanilla

1. Place the sugar and water in a heavy-based saucepan, and bring to the boil.
2. After boiling for approximately 1 to 2 minutes, add the vanilla and stir through.

Serving Suggestion:

Use over Pikelets / Pancakes (see recipe in the 'Desserts' section) topped with icing sugar or over Poppy Seed Cake (see recipe in the 'Baking' section). Also good in marinades if you've run out of the real thing.

Acknowledgements and Thanks

Steve - My darling husband for your support and encouragement during the long journey, and for converting the Australian measurements for readers in other countries.

Brandon and Caitie - For your willingness to be my 'guinea pigs' and try new recipes. Thanks also for the many times you said "You HAVE to put this one in your book!"

Margie (Mum) - For being a test kitchen, for your input, and for being the wonderful mum that you are.

Diane (Mum) - For your suggestions, inspiration and encouragement. As mothers-in-law go, you rock!

Joy - You are a wonderful grandma, and I am proud and privileged to include both some unchanged and some modified versions of your recipes that you have passed down the generations.

Aunty Carolyn and my late Aunty Sophia - For passing down the family recipes for Bub's biscuits with a practical demonstration. You inspired me to buy my Kenwood Chef – who would have known that it was just the beginning of a longer and more delicious journey.

Cathy - For allowing me to play with your vanilla slice recipe and "de-egg" it.

Alix – For sharing recipes that I could adapt.

Claire - For editing, testing and tasting during the book's early stages.

My wider family and many friends - Thanks for the encouragement and making sure I actually finished this book.

And to my Lord – Thank you that I survived many serious anaphylactic reactions, and was able to write this book to help others do the same.

Useful Internet references on food intolerances and allergies

Why many Americans have food allergies

www.cbsnews.com/news/food-allergies-in-america-new-report-shellfish-peanut-dairy

Food Allergy Research and Education

www.foodallergy.org/life-food-allergies/food-allergy-101/facts-and-statistics

Guidelines for the Diagnosis and Management of Food Allergy in the United States

www.ncbi.nlm.nih.gov/pmc/articles/PMC4241964

Allergy and Anaphylaxis Australia

www.allergyfacts.org.au/allergy-anaphylaxis/food-allergy

Australian Society of Clinical Immunology and Allergy (ASCIA)

www.allergy.org.au/patients/food-allergy/food-allergy

Allergic Living Magazine

www.allergicliving.com

Food Intolerance Network (by Sue Dengate)

www.fedup.com.au

Royal Prince Alfred Hospital Allergy Unit

www.slhd.nsw.gov.au/RPA/Allergy/resources/foodintol/ffintro.html

Food Standards Australia and New Zealand

www.foodstandards.gov.au/consumer/foodallergies/allergies/Pages/default.aspx

The Healthy Food Guide - Special Diet

www.healthyfoodguide.com.au/recipes/Allergy-friendly-recipes

Eating with food allergies

www.eatingwithfoodallergies.com

Food Allergies Recipe Box

www.foodallergiesrecipebox.com

Essential Kids - Allergies and Illness

www.essentialkids.com.au/health/allergies-illness

Kids with Food Allergies - a division of the Asthma and Allergy Foundation of America

www.kidswithfoodallergies.org/page/welcome.aspx

The above links are active at the time of publishing.

Back cover

A collection of 100 family-friendly low allergy recipes. Especially written for people with salicylate intolerance, and allergies to egg, tomato, onion, beef, potato, gelatin and yeast.

From tasty main dishes like casseroles, pies and stir fry dishes, to mud cake and eggless pancakes.

This is sure to be a treat for the whole family.

A must for anyone with food allergies or food intolerances.

Printed in the United States
By Bookmasters